Mamuka

בית ספר גבוה בית יעקב דשיקגו
Bais Yaakov High School of Chicago

3550 West Peterson Avenue · Chicago, Illinois 60659

This book is a poignant personal memoir of a woman whose nobility of character (*midos tovos*), concern for others (*gemillas chassadim*) and modesty in dress and conduct (*tznius*) made her a prototype of the true *"Yiddishe Mamma."* It is presented to you by Bais Yaakov High School of Chicago, the newest link in the golden chain of Torah education for girls started by Sarah Schenirer in Poland over seventy years ago and continued by Rebbetzin Vichna Kaplan in America. Bais Yaakov, headed by Rebbetzin Shulamis Keller, herself a student of Rebbetzin Kaplan, is dedicated to the propostion that the type of woman portrayed in **Mamuka** should not become an extinct species.

The school's goal is to develop a *derech hachayim*, a Torah sense of direction,which will help prepare the girls for the vast and varied experiences of life. This is to be achieved by internalization of all that is studied into the character, emotions and actions of the *talmidos*. A dedicated staff of dynamic, experienced and committed teachers offers a high-level educational program, both in Torah and in general studies. Individualized personal attention is given to each girl in order to help her develop her maximum potential. An extensive vibrant program of extracurricular activities is designed to develop useful skills and talents and to make the girls' school experience more enjoyable and fulfilling.

Your support will help develop today's young Jewish girl into tomorrow's *aishes chayil*—woman of valor.

Mamuka

A MEMOIR BY
GITEL GREENHUT

PUBLISHERS

New York · London · Jerusalem

Published and distributed
in the U.S., Canada and overseas by
C.I.S. Publishers and Distributors
180 Park Avenue, Lakewood, New Jersey 08701
(908) 905-3000 Fax: (908) 367-6666

Distributed in Israel by
C.I.S. International (Israel)
Rechov Mishkalov 18
Har Nof, Jerusalem
Tel: 02-538-935

Distributed in the U.K. and Europe by
C.I.S. International (U.K.)
1 Palm Court, Queen Elizabeth Walk
London, England N16
Tel: 01-809-3723

Book and cover design: Deenee Cohen
Typography: Shami Reinman

ISBN 1-56062-072-2 hard cover

I dedicate this book to
my dear parents
in loving memory

Gitele

Foreword

MY MOTHER LEFT THIS WORLD AT THE AGE OF SEVENTY-FIVE after an illness of three and a half months. The sad duty of going through and disposing of her possessions was almost unbearable. The tears came and couldn't be stopped.

It was painful to handle the embroidered short-sleeved undershirt she wore to make sure nothing showed through her modest garments. Spotless, neat, but patched, the undershirt was the same one she had worn to America. She did not think it necessary to buy new clothes; the money could be given to some poor person who needed it more. For Mamuka measured life's value by how much she could do for others. Talented, wise and charismatic, she used all her blessings for *chessed*.

I wish I could fill these pages with happy events and laughter. Unfortunately, there was little to smile about. Of the loss of her firstborn, Mamuka said, "I didn't think I could survive it." Thirty odd years later, after losing three more children in the Holocaust, she said, "May Hashem try us with less pain than we can bear."

Mamuka possessed tremendous inner strength. With humor and *emunah*, she raised seven children alone in Hungary while my father was supporting the family from America.

Among her things was a ledger in which she kept her charity accounts and wrote sixty pages about her life; she never had time to write more. When I realized how much she wanted to write about her life, I made a silent promise. But the years go by faster than we like. The everyday struggle of raising children, the everyday *nachas* and heartache, and the fact that I am not a writer, somehow always pushed that promise to the back of my mind. But after twenty-six years of procrastinating, I began. Although I doubt that I have the talent to do justice to her memory, I tried my best.

There are so many memories. As I wrote, sometimes my heart surged with an exceptionally warm feeling at remembrance; at other times, an almost unbearable sadness overtook me.

Most of what I wrote is from my own experience. Some things, especially from earlier years, I heard from Mamuka, others from my older siblings. In addition, many strangers have told me about my mother. It is heartwarming to hear people talking about her even after all these years. Some said that when she rang the bell, on her regular rounds collecting *tzedakah*, they would not let her climb the stairs; instead, they took the money down to her. A special *berachah* to those who helped her in her good works.

Giving *tzedakah* and helping people was a way of life in my parents' home in Europe, and later in America, and I can proudly say that we try our best to follow in their footsteps. Our own good deeds, from marrying off orphans to my sister Feige's baking apples and yams for elderly people, are the direct result of what we saw at home.

I would like to thank Tamar Chanan, a very dear neighbor and good friend, for typing my entire manuscript. I would also like to thank my editor Esther Van Handel for putting up with me through the shaping and polishing of my book. Last, but not least, thanks to my dear husband and children for their constant encouragement.

Hungary

Chapter One

MY MOTHER—WE CALLED HER MAMUKA—WAS BORN IN A SMALL Hungarian town of Mad. The youngest of the six Brown children, she was vivacious and outgoing.

Zeide Brown, a wholesale dealer of fowl, was poor in worldly possessions but rich in Torah. Although he did not wear a *shtreimel*, the mark of a rabbi or *shochet* in most of Hungary, it was well known that he was a *talmid chacham* who never wasted a minute that could have been spent learning. His business was conducted through a small window at the front of the house. Inside, underneath the window, stood a small table on which the *Gemara* was a permanent fixture. Sometimes Bubby would wake up in the middle of the night and see him swaying tiredly over the *Gemara*. "You are wasting a good candle," she would say jokingly, and gently urge him to retire for a few hours.

Bubby Brown gave birth to three children in her first few years of marriage, and lost all of them in infancy. When she was expecting the fourth, she was advised to give the child away to strangers to raise because it was believed that she didn't have *mazal* to raise children. Sure enough, the baby boy was given to a neighbor who was a close friend. Bubby watched from afar, with an aching heart, as Avraham Meyer grew. Fortunately, she had four other children in quick succession who thrived under her careful upbringing. Her only son was returned to the family fold at the age of six, a beautiful, sturdy youngster with a keen interest in learning.

Avraham Meyer learned in the Mader Yeshivah. The girls were raised to be what was at that time termed *"Chassidic."*

Mamuka was not required to do much housework because at the age of thirteen she began sewing for the family. With the help of her older sisters, she practically dressed the entire family. She sewed shirts and underwear for the men, and she was only sorry that she could not tailor suits as well. At sixteen, she undertook to sew a wedding gown for a poor *kallah*, although the family tried to talk her out of it for fear she might ruin the material. Throughout her life, she continued to undertake bold tasks without fear of failure; an idea once born was immediately put into action.

When Zeide fell ill with typhus, for some reason he kept praying to Hashem for a gift of six more years of life. Bubby and Uncle Avraham Meyer admonished him to ask for enough years to marry off his children, but he would not change his plea. He died exactly six years later, leaving two unmarried children. His body was taken into the *shul*, and *hakafos* were made with his *aron*—an honor reserved for Torah scholars. The small table that had held his *Gemara* was moved into the *shul* and kept there.

More than fifty years later, a *rosh yeshivah* in Williamsburg told my nephew Shimon that he was learning in the Mader Yeshivah when Zeide died. He recalled that the Mader Rav had requested that only those who had purified themselves in the *mikveh* handle Zeide's body or the *aron*.

My father, whom we children called Tatika, was related to half of Europe's *rabbanim* through his mother's family.

His father's grandfather, Great-grandfather Weinstock, was a tall, good-looking man with a long beard who sported a silk top hat, spats and a silver-headed ebony cane. When he walked down the street, people turned their heads to take a second look. Great-grandfather owned land in Hungary's Tokay mountain region. He was the proud holder of a letter awarding him the title of baron, a rare honor for a Jew.

Grandfather inherited the land and title. But before Great-grandfather died, he told Grandfather that he did not want his descendants to hold on to the land because he was afraid the affluence might hurt their *Yiddishkeit*. So Grandfather opened a grocery store in Ujhel.

In his spare time, he would learn. Often, when the bell over the front door of the store rang, Grandmother would run from the kitchen, wiping her hand on her apron, to wait on a customer so as not to disturb Grandfather's learning. Yet he was never too immersed in his studies to see that the customers got their money's worth in weight and fresh merchandise.

Chapter Two

TATIKA WAS AS QUIETLY RESERVED AS MAMUKA WAS VIVACIOUS
and outgoing. Yet they had a special regard for each other
that was apparent even to strangers, a regard that was to
endure even when fate separated them for long periods of
time.

By the time my parents married, Uncle Avraham Meyer
had already settled in Szemihaly. He was doing well in the
wine and liquor trade. On his advice, my parents came to
settle there.

Tatika made a very comfortable living as a watchmaker,
and they fixed up a three-room apartment with all the
comforts that were then available. When Mamuka first started
cooking, she prepared all the ingredients, put them in the
pot, set the pot on the range and forgot to put a match to the
kindling wood underneath. Eventually, though, she became

an expert at cooking and baking.

When their first child was born, their joy was boundless. Unfortunately, the little one suffered a crib death before the *bris*. "I didn't think I could survive it," Mamuka later wrote. Little did Mamuka know that this was just the first taste of her "life full of tragedy," as she called it.

Life went on. Tatika had steady work, and Mamuka was occupied with making their little home pretty. Although it was far from the center of town, family and friends visited often. Some of them said, "All that is needed in the Weinstock house is a cradle."

Hashem was good to them, and in the third year of their marriage Mamuka gave birth to her first little girl—Chayah Sarah. Then Mamuka had another little girl. Her name was Raidl.

When Mamuka was expecting her third child, the trouble started. Tatika was called up for active duty in the army. On the army pittance, he could not support his family. The little they had saved was quickly used up, and he was forced to take help from his own family and from Uncle. It was a bitter pill to swallow.

At the birth of her first two children, Mamuka had her mother with her. For the birth of Eisik Dovid, her third child, Bubby was ill. A few days before the *bris*, Bubby passed away. Mamuka sensed that something was amiss when she was told that Uncle, who was supposed to be the *mohel*, was away in Austria on business. She could not believe he would take a trip just then and leave her to find a *mohel* herself. Right after Eisik's *bris*, her sisters left for Mad. Mamuka begged them to let her know how her mother was. When she didn't hear from anyone, she guessed the sad truth.

One night after the *bris*, Tatika came home. But Mamuka's happiness quickly turned to fear. Tatika told her that he had deserted. "I want to go to America," he said. "Please give me your blessing."

Mamuka refused. "I would rather wash other people's laundry and clean their homes than let you go. I beg you, go back and serve your time. We'll manage somehow until your release."

But Tatika did not report back for duty, as Mamuka found out when the police came looking for him.

Wearing brass-buttoned uniforms and helmets with tall feathers, the *zsandarn* looked formidable on their magnificent mounts. These arrogant policemen were accountable to no one. Any excuse whatsoever was enough to arrest a man, beat him mercilessly and send him to forced labor in "Siberia." (There was, of course, no region called Siberia in Hungary, but we all knew what the dreaded expression meant.) When you saw them coming, you either bowed down or ducked behind a tree.

When Tatika deserted, the *zsandarn* began to come to the house daily. Then they stayed away for weeks, only to reappear suddenly, hoping to catch their prey off guard. Once, when Tatika showed up in the middle of the night, Mamuka told him not to come again because he would be executed if they found him.

Mamuka did not know where Tatika was hiding. The few letters she received were mailed from different places. Once, before *Sukkos*, Tatika made the mistake of sending a bushel of grapes. She had to go pick it up at the post office. The postmaster told Mamuka that Tatika's name was on a "wanted" poster.

"That's impossible!" said Mamuka. "My husband went to join up in 1912. I hope nothing happened to him."

Seeing how upset Mamuka was, the postmaster said, "Maybe I was mistaken."

Mamuka had forebodings that the *zsandarn* would come that night, and she went to bed with all her clothes on.

They did come that night. They searched all over the little house for Tatika, without success.

"It would be best for you," they told Mamuka, "if you told us where he is."

"If I knew where he is," she replied, "I would report him immediately. He left me with three children!"

She later referred to that time as "my night of horrors."

One snowy *Shabbos* morning, a letter came from Tatika. It was lying on the table when, through the window, Mamuka saw the *zsandarn* approaching. Frightened as she was, she had the presence of mind to throw the letter into the fire. Mamuka was warned again that Tatika would be shot if he did not turn himself in.

Mamuka began to notice that her gentile neighbors asked too many questions when they saw the mailman coming, and she knew they would gladly report her. She made up her mind to go after Tatika. Somehow, she would find him and warn him of the danger. Whatever the consequences, at least she would not be around for the terrible visits of the *zsandarn*.

One day, Uncle came with a message from Tatika, once again asking her to let him go to America. Mamuka forced the information of Tatika's whereabouts from Uncle. He was heading for Ujhel.

Against Uncle's advice, Mamuka went about systematically breaking up her warm little nest. She sold the furnishings and whatever else she could. The rest—dishes, linens, bedding and clothes—she packed in a hired wagon. The driver of the team, one of Uncle's hired hands, was instructed to go to Mad and to unload everything at the home of one of Mamuka's sisters.

Early on a very cold March morning of 1913, Mamuka

started out with a baby in her arms, two children tugging at her skirt, Bertha, a young cousin who lived with her and helped with the children, and various bundles. They changed trains three times, with long waits in between. Since the cars were crowded with soldiers, the family did not always have seats.

Finally, long after dark, they arrived in Ujhel. Mamuka was swollen with milk, for she had not been able to nurse the baby regularly. The children were tired and cranky. Taking hold of Chayah Sarah's hand, Mamuka felt the child shivering with cold. She asked Sonia to go find a buggy to take them into town. Then, leaving her bundles on the platform, Mamuka looked for someplace to take the shaking child for some warmth. With the baby in her arms and the two children holding on to her skirt, she opened the first door she saw and entered.

There, with a soldier guarding him, stood Tatika.

Tatika's surprise reflected Mamuka's astonishment as she asked, "What are you doing here?"

Tatika picked up the shivering child, and all Mamuka's bravery melted into tears. "I gave up everything," she said, "to come and warn you to go to a bigger city where they would not find you."

Turning to the soldier, Mamuka begged him to let Tatika go.

Tatika took Mamuka aside. "The soldier guarding me is Jewish," he said. "Through the long hours of waiting, he turned his back many times, but I did not try to escape. I do not want to run anymore. You were right. I'll have to serve my time and hope for the best. The soldier told me his report will state that I turned myself in."

After what seemed like a very short time, the guard said, "We must leave now."

Mamuka's pleas that they take the next train were in vain.

"Take the children to my parents," said Tatika. "I'll write as soon as I can."

When Mamuka finally knocked on the window of Grandparents' home, she found them worriedly debating how to let her know about Tatika's arrest. Mamuka felt sorry for them, but all she could think about then was a warm bed and sleep.

Tatika's letter came as promised. He wrote that the guard took the wrong train. When he noticed his mistake, they were an hour away from Ujhel. They spent the night at the depot in that small town. Mamuka shed bitter tears. What it would have meant to both of them to spend those few hours together! Then more than ever, she realized that no one can shape his own destiny.

Mamuka stayed with my grandparents over *Pesach*. But as gracious as they were, Mamuka realized that she could not impose on them any longer. For the hundredth time, she called herself a fool for giving up her home.

After *Pesach*, at her sister's invitation, she spent a short time in Mad in the house where she was born. By then, her sister also had a growing family, so it was not any easier there although everyone was very generous. She was overjoyed when Uncle agreed to help her reestablish her home in Szemihaly. At that time, having her own home again was her greatest wish.

Mamuka returned to Szemihaly, to a little house in the center of town with two large rooms, a summer kitchen and an outhouse at the end of a big yard. Uncle was able to bribe influential people higher up, so Tatika was sent to work with farm machinery to help the war effort rather than to the front. Now and then, he came home on leave.

Mamuka tried to earn money by rendering fat from the various fowl to sell. Many hours of backbreaking work went into each twenty-gallon can of fat.

One morning, some finance officers came and confiscated two cans because she had no license to sell the product. Mamuka was devastated. "If and when you bring a letter of release from the Office of Licenses," they told her, "you will get them back."

The Office of Licenses was located in a nearby town. Although she was at the end of her ninth month, Mamuka quickly hired a horse and cart from a gentile neighbor and rode to the office. As she rode back into Szemihaly with the required document in her hand, smugly imagining the discomfiture of the finance officers, the horse suddenly bolted and got partly loose from its harness. The driver jumped down and tried to keep the beast in check. Failing that, he unharnessed it. As the cart came free, it rolled and tipped forward. By some miracle, Mamuka landed on her feet, the document like a flag in her hand.

The driver wanted his money. Mamuka refused to pay, arguing that he had not gotten her where she had to go. By then, a sizable crowd had gathered, including Uncle Avraham Meyer.

"Thank Hashem that you are not hurt. Pay the driver," said Uncle. "The town hall is within easy walking distance. Come, let's go."

The crowd went along to see the outcome of this exciting event. Eager hands helped her carry the precious cargo she redeemed.

Mamuka crowned the day by giving birth to a healthy girl, whom she named Feige.

In the next few years, Mamuka gave birth to Channah and Rivkah.

When the First World War ended, Tatika was finally released from the army. But there was no work for a watchmaker. Who could afford to have watches fixed? He did what he could, going to larger towns during the week and coming home for *Shabbos*.

One day, a friend of Mamuka's came over to show off her new Persian lamb coat. Tatika happened to be home at the time. When the friend left, he told Mamuka, "You should be wearing a coat like that."

Tatika was very bitter about not being able to provide enough food to give the children, let alone the luxuries he felt she deserved. The determination to go to America became stronger every year. He tried to work at everything he could lay his hands on, but still could not provide nearly enough.

In 1923, Mamuka gave birth to her last child. I made my appearance very early in the morning, when Feige was about to go milk the cow with the gentile maid. (Since milk was purchased from gentiles a Jewish person was required to be present at milking time.) Tatika told the wide-eyed child that Mamuka had a baby.

"Is it a girl or a boy?" she asked.

Tatika mischievously told her, "It's a boy."

Feige went off happily and regaled whomever she met with the good news that Mamuka had a *yingele*. Everyone found out the truth soon enough, but at least for a short time Tatika escaped being teased for producing a sixth girl. As for me, as long as I was in Szemihaly, one of our neighbors still called me "Gitu-boy."

Whenever Tatika left for another city, Mamuka walked him to the gate to say goodbye, and she always tried to be at the gate when he returned.

The financial situation was so bad at one time that Tatika asked Mamuka if he could sell her diamond ring. Mamuka took the ring off her finger without a word.

"I'll buy you a nicer one," he promised.

Tatika was miserable. Not to be able to provide properly for his family was torture for him.

Chapter Three

ONE NICE MORNING IN MARCH OF 1924, MAMUKA TOOK A LIGHT shawl to walk Tatika once again to the gate before his departure. "Take your coat," he said. "I'd like you to walk me a short way."

Mamuka always knew that a time would come when she would not be able to keep him from going to America, and she felt that this was it.

As they walked out of the gate, they saw Aunt Sureh coming, her arms loaded with baskets full of baking materials. Two weeks before *Purim*, Mamuka always helped her do her baking. So they both knew that Mamuka wouldn't be able to accompany him any further.

Mamuka would never forget the expression on his face when she whispered to him, "Go with my blessing and be *matzliach*."

"I won't be away more than a year," Tatika optimistically assured her.

After Tatika left, Mamuka prepared for *Purim* like in any other year so that we would not feel our loss too much. But one day when she was sitting with the nine-month-old baby on her lap, and her three-year-old, five-year-old and six-year-old standing around her, she broke down and cried. The three older children came home from school and found places around her.

"Please, dear Mamuka, don't cry," Chaya Sarah said. "You have us. Can you imagine how much harder it is for Tatika? He is all alone."

Indeed, Tatika was all alone. He went to Germany, where he had to wait six months to raise enough money to pay for passage on a boat to America.

Meanwhile, Mamuka had a very hard time making ends meet. In an effort to take as little as possible from Uncle and Zeide, she took in some sewing and also raised ducks. In those days vegetable oils were not used, so the fat from those ducks was sold profitably in cities.

At that time, Mamuka also covered her *shaitel* with a *tichel*. To those who asked why, Mamuka explained, "My husband is not home, and I don't want to make myself look pretty for anyone else."

Once he arrived in America, Tatika had no trouble finding work. He was an excellent watchmaker, and in America there were plenty of watches to repair. He started sending money home almost immediately. With his first earnings, he bought Mamuka a beautiful ring with delicate diamond petals.

The money that Tatika sent home from America was budgeted very carefully. Before all the debts were paid up only the absolute necessities were bought. Later, as the planned year turned into three, Mamuka was able to build a large new home from the American money on a lot right next to the old one.

Moving day was something to remember. The new house looked grand after the old one. The toilet was still outdoors, but the summer kitchen was inside and there were more stoves in the house than I had ever seen before. Each of the four big rooms had a wood-burning stove, and the kitchen had a real bread-baking oven with a hump that extended into the woodshed behind the kitchen. A few steps up from the garden was a large, L-shaped veranda running the length of the house. Part of the veranda was designated for a *sukkah*, which we dreamed of using the first time when Tatika came home.

There was also a storefront—a very large area with an entrance and a showcase window—for Tatika's business when he returned. In the meantime, it was a wonderful place to play games, especially on rainy days.

There was another thing in the new house we did not have in the old one—electricity! Mamuka's face was glowing at the thought of having such a tremendous convenience in her home, and it seemed to me that the sadness in her eyes was a little diminished.

The plan for building the house was made by Tatika, and it included a small area designated for a future indoor bathroom. Having gotten used to the comfort of a bathroom in America, he chose to overlook the impossibility of making it a reality. In the meantime, the room was there, so Mamuka put it to good use as a guest room for poor travellers who used to come to our town from time to time to raise money and needed a place to stay overnight. I remember Mamuka giving us a carefully prepared list of addresses and telling us to point out to these travellers the doors on which to knock.

At the time that our new house was being completed, someone in town died and the family decided to move away. Mamuka bought some of the furniture that was put on sale. It was second-hand but grand.

As every piece of furniture was put in place, one of us would say, "Would Tatika like it here?" or "I wonder what Tatika will say when he walks in and sees this." The way we spoke, one would think he was expected to walk in at any minute, or at the latest in a few weeks. Of course, it was just a dream, so we continued having plenty and living without Tatika.

Many people in our town may have thought us lucky and, if given the choice, would have exchanged our lot for their miserably poor existence.

Chapter Four

TO MAMUKA, HER LONELINESS WAS A CHALLENGE TO BE MET head-on. She took the reins in her capable hands with good humor and *emunah*. One thing that helped her avoid self-pity was her charity work.

My earliest conscious memory of Mamuka is from the age of four, when I was playing in the corner of the large living room in our new house with my toys, toys that no other child in our town had. A neighbor and her daughter were talking with Mamuka in low voices.

"Don't worry," Mamuka said in Yiddish. "It will be all right. It will all work out for the best." That was a promise.

Promises like that were not easy to fulfill in those days. Whatever was raised from the townspeople was never enough. When there was a poor *kallah* in town, or any other worthy cause, Mamuka and a lady of her choosing travelled to nearby cities for a few days to collect money. Whenever there was sickness or just no income in a large or small family, there was always help. Mamuka somehow found a way.

When it came to marrying off a young couple, Mamuka spared no effort. The background was almost always the same. A girl from a respectable but very poor family, no father, many younger children, mother eking out a meager living by sewing for people. A young man also from a good family, but–alas!–also poor. He is a *melamed* and ready to marry. Someone in town has an idea. Pretty girl, good-looking boy. Both poor. Why not? The necessary things were provided, and on his small pay as a *melamed*, having no choice, they started out in life without fear of the future.

In those days, a *chassan* and *kallah* did not see each other between the engagement and the wedding; and since there were no telephones, they could not even speak to each other. When I was eight, I carried letters back and forth between one such couple, and felt quite important. But after they warned me repeatedly that no one must know, I began to think that I was doing something wrong; and if it was wrong, Mamuka ought to know about it. So I told her. She just laughed, so I continued delivering.

I remember waking up in the early morning to the flicker of a candle's glow. I crept out of my little bed and into Mamuka's, where she was reciting *Tehillim*. It had to be done early, because after taking care of the family she went around town to visit the sick and make sure the poor had food for breakfast.

Mamuka collected from the rich to give to the poor. She was very careful not to embarrass the recipients. Money was left on a table or chair during a quick visit, stuck through an open window and left on the window sill, or put into a pocket of a used garment being given away. When she sent us to a poor family to deliver some things, Mamuka told us to knock on the door and run away. The gifts of flour, sugar and fat sent out a week before *Purim* were delivered at night.

One winter day, Feige ran in to tell Mamuka that she saw a man going out of our woodshed taking cut wood on a pushcart. Mamuka told her to take no notice of it and not to tell anyone.

One of the families that Mamuka always helped was the Weiners. Mrs. Weiner was as round as she was tall. She came to our town from Budapest with her sickly old husband and five children. When Mr. Weiner had been able to work, he had made enough money to support the family, but unfortunately, that ended with his illness, and their savings were soon consumed. When they left Budapest, they sold all their belongings to cover the move to Szemihaly, where they had relatives. But these cousins were too poor to really help.

When the cousins rented a small house for the Weiners on the lot next to ours, Mrs. Weiner immediately acquired her first friend in town. Mamuka, who always sensed where help was needed, saw the family moving in and promptly sent Chayah Sarah over to see if they needed anything.

After a few days, Mrs. Weiner asked us to call her Tante Rosa, and we did not mind, for in spite of her hardships she was a jolly, lovable lady.

Mamuka asked Uncle Avraham Meyer to speak to our *rosh yeshivah* about a job for Mr. Weiner. Uncle got him a job, and for a short time, he was able to teach. But then he took to his bed and passed away soon after.

Mamuka used to send me over to see how Tante Rosa was doing. She found out that Tante Rosa would have liked to earn money by sewing, but she did not have a machine. When Mamuka got a new sewing machine, she kept the old one and gave the new one to Tante Rosa. "If she is to earn a living by sewing," said Mamuka, "then she needs the better machine."

Many times, I found Tante Rosa humming a little tune as she pumped the pedal, and I would sing along. The only time I saw Tante Rosa without a smile was when a needle broke, or when she made a mistake cutting and ruined a piece of material. There were bad days when she had to search for change three or four times to buy a new needle. If she didn't find any money, I was sent to "borrow" from Mamuka. Since her boys were in *yeshivah* and her daughter did the house-work while she sewed, I came in handy running for needles. After Mamuka opened the store, she gave out merchandise to Tante Rosa and others like her who had no money, and recorded the transaction in a big book.

Tante Rosa was happy that her beautiful daughter married the *melamed*, and a year later, they had their first boy. When we left for America, Tante Rosa cried the loudest.

The cobbler was another of Mamuka's "clients." He was a *talmid chacham* who was very poor but refused to accept charity. When he came to pay back money he had borrowed, Mamuka would say, "You must have forgotten that you already paid."

Sometimes the ruse worked. But if he insisted, Mamuka took the money back rather than make him feel bad.

Mamuka chose workers more for their need than for their ability. She would send me to the cobbler with shoes that no longer fit any of us, because fixing them gave the cobbler work and meager earnings. Amidst torn cartons and broken crates, with his tools arranged around him, he sat holding the shoe he was fixing between his knees. I watched in wonder as he put the wooden nails in his mouth and then took them out again. I couldn't figure out how he knew where to put those nails without moving his eyes from the open *sefer* on the stool before him.

I was there once when the door in the back of the shop opened and one of his many daughters brought in bread and soup. Without changing positions, he took the cup of water and washed his hands. He made the *berachah* on the bread, then kept looking into the *sefer* while he ate. The only change was that now he held the bowl on his knees instead of the shoe. For a long time, I thought he was not able to stand, until one day I noticed him walking to *shul* with his *tallis* under his arm.

Mamuka eventually found people who could use those shoes. She never threw anything away. "What one person can't use," she said, "others may be happy with." She always made sure that the things given away were in good condition.

The tinsmith's eldest daughter was old enough to work. Since she had no training of any sort, her parents decided to hire her out to a good family as a live-in housekeeper. That would make one less mouth to feed, and she might even send some of her earnings home. The arrangements were made by mail on recommendation, and she landed an advantageous position in Budapest with a nice family. In fact, the family were so nice that they sent a ticket to the mother with an invitation to come for a weekend and see for herself that her daughter was fine.

Tante Irma (we called all the ladies in town "Tante"), the tinsmith's wife, was thrilled about the trip. This would be the first time she had been out of town since her arrival in Szemihaly after her marriage. There was only one problem. She did not own a single dress nice enough for a trip to the big city. She came to Mamuka in tears, saying, "I want to look decent."

Since ready-made clothes were nonexistent, and there was no time to have something sewn, Mamuka ran around town finding out who had a dress the right size and was willing to lend it. At last, a decent wardrobe was assembled. A dress for travel and another one for *Shabbos* were borrowed, and a pair of good-looking, serviceable shoes were purchased in the local shoe store (Tante Irma needed shoes anyway).

"What about a robe for when I get up *Shabbos* morning?" asked Tante Irma.

"You don't need one," said Mamuka. "Put on the *Shabbos* dress as soon as you get up."

Tante Irma, however, was not satisfied with this advice. She hurried to my newly married cousin Fritzy, who had bought part of her trousseau in a big town, and asked if she could borrow a robe.

Fritzy ran to consult Mamuka.

"I would gladly lend it to her," she said. "But how would it look for a woman whose daughter is in service to show up in such a fancy robe?"

"Of course, that won't do," agreed Mamuka.

So Mamuka bustled around town again looking for a woman the right size who was willing to lend a second dress. Finally, to everyone's relief, Mamuka managed to convince Tante Irma to take along two *Shabbos* dresses instead of a dress and a robe.

Our yard was partly flower, partly vegetable garden. Between the summer kitchen and the outhouse, there was a large area where we used to play. Just beyond the fence that ended our property was the barnyard of the highest official of our town hall. We children were forever hanging on top of that fence. The entertainment was endless–horses, fowl of all kinds, goats and cows. That fence was the gate to a child's paradise. But there was something else there, too. A lot of diplomacy went over that fence in the form of *matzos* on *Pesach*, wine and cakes on *Purim* and *cholent* on *Shabbos* (carried by the gentile maid). When Mamuka needed a favor for someone in town and knew she could not approach the official directly, his wife was approached. She, in turn, spoke to her husband, and endless trouble was avoided. It didn't always work, but it was worth a try.

Once a large truck passing through town developed some mechanical problem. The driver stopped to fix it, leaving behind some greasy paper in front of someone's house. Early the next morning, the *zsandarn* passed by. When they saw the paper, they arrested the owner of the house for violating the cleanliness law. The man pleaded that it was too early in the morning for him to have gone out and seen the paper.

"If you do not go with us peaceably," they replied, "you will be taken forcibly."

So he went along, a pathetic figure plodding beside the horses. One of his children came running in tears to our house. Mamuka went to the fence and asked one of the yard workers to call "the lady." She came, and they exchanged some whispered words. Towards evening, the arrested man came home to his family.

Whenever we had a nice duck or goose liver it was always sent to one of the more important gentiles for future favors. Once when there was chicken skin melting to make schmaltz, the wife of a big shot from the junior army who was in the store remarked that something smelled very good. Mamuka took her back to the kitchen and gave her a plateful of fried chicken skin and a raw duck liver.

One man was taken in for selling his military caps for two pennies more than the gentile store. He was going to be sent to "Siberia" for price hiking. Over the fence, Mamuka found out details. A cash bribe was involved, and that was considered treason. Notwithstanding, Mamuka did not hesitate to arrange it. He was spared forced labor in "Siberia," but the beating he received left him lame for life.

Chapter Five

WHEN MAMUKA WENT TO *SHUL* ON *SHABBOS*, WE TAGGED ALONG
to *daven* a little and play with the other children who came
there for the same reason. After the meal we could sleep or
not, as we pleased, but we had to be quiet so as not to disturb
those who wanted to rest. In the summer, we had to be home
at a certain time for *Perek* and *Minchah*. There was plenty of
time for play.

One *Shabbos* when we had no gentile maid, as the help had
all left to do field work, I had to carry a laden tray of food to
a sick old man who would otherwise have gone hungry all
Shabbos. The tray, almost as large as me, was supported by
Raidl, who was too old to carry.

Sometimes, we slept in the summer kitchen because the
house was turned over to guests who came to Szemihaly on
special occasions. After our old rabbi died, the Satmar Rebbe

campaigned for Reb Lipele to fill his place. The streets were crowded with strangers from far and near. The *rebbe* stayed in Uncle's house, and we had about thirty people for *Shabbos*. When Reb Lipele came to Szemihaly, Uncle brought him over to our house for *melaveh malkah*. Mamuka, in her element when called on to prepare for special occasions, served hot borscht, potatoes and many different kind of *kugels*. She put her whole heart into it.

Winter *Shabossim* had their own special flavor. As short as Friday was, Mamuka made time to make paper thin *motzelach* for the hot chicken soup "*lechavod Shabbos*." I can still smell the pungent garlic we rubbed into it.

During the long Friday nights, neighbors—women and children—gathered at our home after the meal for companionship. *Shabbos* days went fast, and my fun began at *shalishudis* time.

Late *Shabbos* afternoon, when it got dark inside as well as out, we started to play "Fire," a game Mamuka made up. The younger children were eager to start, and the older ones played along to please the younger ones by increasing the din. One had to say in a monotone, "Fire . . . fire . . . fire." Another had to say, "Where? . . . where? . . . where?" Still another had to chant, "Water . . . water . . . water." I was the bell. That part had a certain fascination, because when there was a fire in town, bells tolled in the tower to alert the fire department and the townspeople. The sound of those bells sent many children scurrying to take cover behind their mother's skirts. Channah used to turn white as chalk from fright. So I chanted with special fervor, "Bungalla . . . bungalla . . . bungalla," imitating the sound of bells, beginning softly and slowly reaching a crescendo.

There was good reason for letting the people know when there was a fire. By the time the horses were harnessed to the one tank of water and the hose, a whole row of straw-roofed dwellings could burn to the ground. So the people would form a fire brigade until the firemen arrived. I was once part of a chain passing pails of water from someone's well to the fire. In fact, the entire Jewish population was there passing those heavy pails. A row of peasant huts was burning, and the Jews were expected to help. When I came home my clothes were unsalvageable. The soot washed out, but an acrid odor remained. Washing my hands and face was not enough. I needed a proper bath. (In those days, proper baths were too difficult to take more than once a week. Water had to be heated and lugged to the wooden tub. It was hard work.)

Never did Mamuka forget those in need, especially when a *Yom Tov* was approaching. She had a list of people from whom she collected *Rosh Chodesh gelt*. In many cases it was only change, but she believed that a lot of a little added up.

One *Purim*, Mamuka dressed up Feige, Channah and their friend as Haman, Achashverosh and Esther. She worked on their *Purim shpiel* with them until it was letter perfect. Then, armed with a list of addresses, they went out to raise money for the poor for *Pesach*. Another time she dressed us as flower girls to go collecting. Wearing artificial flowers in our hair and pinned to our clothes, we sang a little song, with a lot of success.

When Mamuka baked for *Purim*, she handed a bowl or a spoon with a little extra left on the bottom to one of us to lick. We used to wipe our plates also, so that no drop of food was left over. Mamuka was always very careful not to let us waste any kind of food. Even now, I can't understand how people can throw out a piece of bread.

The first time I was trusted with the treasured porcelain cake dish that was used only for *Purim*, I dropped it. The dish broke, and the elegantly arranged cakes went flying all over. I was grounded for the rest of the day.

Matzoh baking was a communal undertaking from *Purim* until *Pesach*. There were some women rolling dough for pay, but mostly one family helped the other. The children measured and supplied the flour and water, a task I found boring. My day was made when the men let me carry the *matzos* to the *gregger* table and the oven. The family who baked that day provided lunch, and each tried to outdo the others with food that was inexpensive but well prepared. Mamuka always baked more than the family's need. Some of our neighbors prepared three *matzos* a day for each child, and the children knew that if they wanted more, Mamuka would give them.

As everywhere, *Pesach* was a special *Yom Tov* for us, with many memories associated with it—the house getting a cleaning from cellar to attic; the excitement of bringing the dishes down from the attic and admiring again and again the gold pattern on the plates and the special little bowls that we children used for *matzos* with milk.

Even if we did not get new clothes for other holidays, for *Pesach* there were always new things to wear. My shiny patent leather shoes with pink socks waiting in the closet were almost as pleasant to think about as getting a letter from Tatika.

At candle lighting time, I watched Mamuka without understanding her freely flowing tears. I always asked her whom all the candles were for. Mamuka lit a candle for every one of her children, even the first baby whom she lost.

Our table was covered for *Yom Tov*, but no one would sit at it. We had our *Sedarim* at the home of Uncle Avraham Meyer. The table spanned two large rooms, and the majesty of Uncle sitting at its head defies description. I had many uncles, all nice, but Mamuka's only brother was the father figure in my young life and I loved him dearly. Instead of making us feel sad that Tatika wasn't with us, Mamuka let us understand that it was a special honor to share *Sedarim* with Uncle.

There was order at the table. The only time we burst out laughing was when Aunt Sureh, who didn't have teeth, pounded her *matzos* in a mortar and pestle so she could eat enough for *Hamotzi*. Although every small child sat next to an older child for proper discipline, Uncle's carefully measured *marror* usually ended up under the table, no matter how watchful the older girls were.

One year, when Eisik was told to ask the Four Questions, he rose and said seriously, "I would like to ask five questions."

Everyone laughed, and our cousins teased him good-naturedly.

Eisik did not respond. He just stood there, his face set in determination. Uncle waited until things quieted down a little, and then said, "If the child says he has five questions, then maybe he does. Let him ask."

Everyone's eyes were on Eisik. In a clear, calm voice he said, "My first question is: Why do I have to ask you these questions and not my own father?" Then he broke down and cried.

All eyes turned to Mamuka, who sat there quietly, tears coursing down her face.

After that, whenever we heard *Kiddush* or *Havdalah*, the question was always there: Why not my father?

On *Rosh Hashanah*, we were dispatched to watch a baby or sit with a sick person so that young mothers or the family of the ill could go to *shul*. Mamuka did not go out into the street except to *shul* and back. She did not talk unless absolutely necessary, or to keep impressing on us how holy those days were. Throughout *Aseres Yemei Teshuvah*, we walked around on tiptoe and talked in whispers.

One *Elul*, when Eisik was twelve years old, he gathered planks and pieces of wood to build a *sukkah*. Until then, he had always eaten in the *sukkah* of Uncle or our neighbors. Mamuka supplied him with a hammer and nails. Eager neighborhood kids lent a hand, and within days, a structure of sorts was standing. It was duly admired by family and friends. Feige, always practical, tested its durability by giving it a push. I can still hear Eisik's heart-rending cries when it fell over.

Mamuka tried not to cry with us over our disappointments, but to teach us to stand up to life's trials. "If a child's push could topple it," she told Eisik, "then it wasn't strong enough to begin with."

That's when Mamuka decided to begin using the *sukkah* that was part of the veranda, even though Tatika was not home.

We had loads of fun. It was a family undertaking. Although I was too young to do anything really constructive, Mamuka did not leave me out. She gave me scraps of shiny colored paper, scissors and paste, and I was in business. To this day that early enthusiasm remains with me, and before *Yom Tov* I always try to make something new and different to enhance the beauty of the *sukkah*. Even taking off the decorations after *Sukkos* and carefully preserving them for the next year was in a way exciting.

Mamuka instilled in us a very special feeling for Yom Tov. The words *"lekovod Gutt"* (in honor of G-d) were always on her lips. Then one of us would mention Tatika. Whatever we did *lekovod Gutt* was somehow always tied in with saying something about my father.

On *Yom Tov*, we got dressed in our finest clothes to go to *shul*. We would stand around in front admiring each other's dresses and sometimes even being a little jealous.

At first, Mamuka *davened* in the big *shul*, a beautiful building with a high dome. I could stare endlessly at the walls and ceilings with their beautiful paintings and stained glass windows. Each *Yom Tov* brings a special memory of that House of G-d. On *Yom Kippur* a tall taper burned on everyone's stand during *Kol Nidre*. On *Simchas Torah*, from the ladies' gallery, we watched the energetic dancing with the Torah. On *Shavuos*, the greens and flowers everywhere transformed the *shul* into an enchanted garden. It was truly magical.

In later years, Mamuka changed over to the humbler atmosphere of the *bais medrash*. Whereas in *shul* the women wore colorful dresses and hats, in the *bais medrash* on *Rosh Hashanah* and *Yom Kippur* the ladies wore white from head to toe. And they cried. Once, when I was *davening*, I told Mamuka I would like to cry, but the tears didn't come. "Why can't I cry?" I asked.

"My dear child," she answered, "crying does not come on command. When there is reason to cry, the tears come unbidden."

Just as Mamuka inspired in us a glowing feeling for *Pesach*, *Sukkos* and the other *Yamim Tovim*, so did she impress upon us the meaning of *Tishah b'Av*. In a gathering of family and friends, her reading of *Eichah* drew tears from old and young.

Chapter Six

WHEREVER MAMUKA WAS DURING THE DAY, SHE WAS always home when it was time for the mailman to come to our house. Sometimes when we did not get mail for longer than usual, she even went out into the street to see if he was coming.

I knew if there was a letter from America, just by watching her face as she scanned the mail. We continued to talk about Tatika coming home, but it became more and more like a dream.

Mamuka had to accept the fact that her little Eisik was growing up very quickly and would soon be *bar mitzvah*. After that, he would have to be sent off to learn in the best *yeshivah*. Unfortunately, he could not attend the famous *yeshivah* in Szemihaly, because boys simply did not stay home after *bar mitzvah*.

Eisik was a serious but fun-loving child and, even at that age, a tremendous moral support for Mamuka. The very thought of not having Eisik around was painful, for Mamuka as well as for all the rest of us. Punishment was not meted out too often or too severely, but when a punishable offense was committed, we would say, "Eisik did it." Usually, we were not believed, but sometimes it actually worked. On those occasions Eisik took it good-naturedly.

It once happened that Mamuka and I had a little run-in, and I suppose I allowed myself to contradict her. Eisik took me aside and gave me an education that made a very deep impression on me. I remember it as clearly as if it had happened just yesterday.

"I don't know what the argument was about," he said. "You may think you are right. But remember, if Mamuka says, 'the milk is black,' the milk is black."

Now, in addition to being intelligent, Mamuka had a sane realism that would never allow her to expect the impossible of us. "The milk is black" was an extreme exaggeration used to impress upon me the importance of listening to Mamuka. In fact, "honor your father and mother" was always firmly impressed upon us. It never occurred to me that it could be otherwise.

Plans were made for Tatika's homecoming in time for the *bar mitzvah* of his only son. The thought of my father coming home gave me a deliciously shivery feeling. But he did not come. The blame for it was ascribed to something called "the Depression," which wiped out all his savings. I, being too young to fully understand the "tragedy," got over the disappointment fast enough. I was happy with the letters and the crates.

Preparations for the great day of the *bar mitzvah* began with joy. In her calm, gentle way, Mamuka did what had to be done to make this *simchah* memorable. The meal, prepared with the aid of family and friends, was appetizing and delicious. The set tables looked like something out of a fairy tale. Mamuka had a way with decorations and ribbons. She did a magnificent job.

It was a festive affair. Uncle Avraham Meyer sat next to Eisik, and Mamuka was everywhere at once. When it came to Eisik's *derashah*, there was such a hush that one could hear the proverbial pin drop.

No one was surprised that it was a brilliant speech, but everyone was awed at the superb delivery. When it seemed that he was finished speaking and the clapping started, he raised his hands to ask for quiet.

The hush returned. He walked over to where Mamuka was standing with the ladies.

"When I had my *bris*, Tatika was in the army," he said in a clear voice. "Now he is in America. I wish from the bottom of my heart that together you and Tatika will take me to the *chupah*."

After the *bar mitzvah*, Eisik left home for the Shoproner Yeshivah. For many days, Mamuka walked around the house as if she had misplaced something. Now there were two people from whom to await letters. During my brother's *yeshivah* years, Mamuka painstakingly learned to write Yiddish in order to be able to correspond with him in that language, even though Eisik was letter perfect in Hungarian and Hebrew.

Sometime after his *bar mitzvah*, Eisik approached Mamuka with a rather unusual request. He asked Mamuka for a second pair of *tefillin*, not a small thing to ask for. He would not say why. Mamuka didn't simply refuse; she said, "I'll have to think about it." As usual, Mamuka went to Uncle to ask for his advice. After speaking to Eisik privately, Uncle told Mamuka to go ahead and buy the second pair. After my father returned home, Eisik apologized for doubting him. Fearing Tatika would neglect his religious practices in America for lack of time, Eisik had used the second pair of *tefillin* for Tatika's sake.

Chapter Seven

MAMUKA OFTEN SANG A HAUNTING SONG ABOUT A YOUNG father who bid his little boy farewell beneath a blooming acacia tree before setting out on a trip around the world. Sighing again and again, he promised to come home when the acacia blossoms would fall. I always asked what happened afterward. Once she finished the song for me. Fifty years passed, and the distinguished gray-haired man returned and stood sighing beneath the acacia tree as he thought of the young son he had left behind. I cried for the young boy, but only years later did I realize that Mamuka associated her own life story with that song.

As I grew up, I learned to accept the sadness in Mamuka's eyes. Even when she laughed, her eyes remained sad. And times of laughter there were. With six girls in the house, there was a lot of coming and going of school friends and neighbors of all ages. Mamuka was able to communicate with them all.

We took frequent trips to the photographers to show Tatika our stages of development. A pencil was put into my hand before I could hold it properly. Mamuka's gentle but firm hand guided mine to write a few words of love to a father so far away, alone without family. I learned the value of a letter at a very early age. I also learned that it was easier to get a letter than to write one.

Although Mamuka tried not to spoil us, she gave us some things that other children did not have so that we would not feel Tatika's absence so keenly.

Even with only letters and pictures for a father, we still had a pretty good childhood. I took advantage of the situation, and the fact that I was very skinny helped. I was fed the "icky" things like Ovomaltine and cod liver oil, but I also got my choice in food. "Give the *pulke* to the child," Mamuka would say.

To get even, Rivkah made believe she had finished her piece of chocolate, and after I had no more, she started licking hers very slowly. I ran howling to Mamuka. I got another piece with the warning, "Don't show it to anyone." After Mamuka realized that I was taunting my sister with it, there were no more extras.

Whenever a crate came with all its goodies—which was often enough—it was practically a holiday.

Those parcels were not simply opened. Mamuka made it almost like a ceremony. She waited until the evening, when all of us were together. Everything lifted out of the package was transformed into an offering of love to one or the other of us.

There were gold rings and watches for us children, wonderful toys, all kinds of nuts that we had never seen before, dried fruits and even a jar of mayonnaise that we had no idea what to do with. A lot of our clothing came from those packages. Whatever Mamuka couldn't remake for us was piled in boxes in the store. Nothing was discarded; what we couldn't use, others could. We had a great time dressing up and making believe in beaded textiles and theatrical-looking jewelry that came out of the crates.

I felt a need to show off my treasures of dolls, balls and other toys that Tatika sent before my friends.

Tatika also sent some of the packages to his parents in Ujhel. Once he sent me a big doll with hair and eyes that opened and closed; she even cried. She was called Alice. Inadvertently, he put Alice into the box to Ujhel.

When Alice finally arrived and Mamuka lifted her out of the box, her dress was torn and some of her hair was missing.

"Don't worry, I'll sew her a new dress," Mamuka said.

Then we noticed a jagged crack from her neck down. I cried as if my heart were breaking, and Mamuka cried with me—but only for a moment.

"Dry your tears," said Mamuka. "I'll mend the doll."

She made a fancy Victorian dress with a high waist and a stiff, fan-like collar to hide the crack. A bonnet partially covered some of the missing hair. When there were friends around, however, I never played with Alice, for fear they might see she was damaged. She sat there in all her glory for people to look at.

I wanted to write to my father about what had happened to Alice, but Mamuka did not let me. "Telling Tatika would serve no purpose other than upsetting him," she said.

Children sometimes made comments about my father's absence, and they cut very deep.

My teacher, upon hearing one such remark, tried to soften the effect by saying in front of the children, "But how lucky you are to have all those nice things!"

On another occasion, Mamuka happened to overhear a child say, "But you have no father!" She took me gently by the hand and led me inside, where she read me Tatika's latest letter. Love and longing poured out of its pages.

Chapter Eight

SZEMIHALY WAS AN AVERAGE TOWN, LIKE HUNDREDS OF OTHERS all over Europe, with about five hundred Jewish families, the more fortunate ones helping the less fortunate. Some were rich. Others were able to make ends meet by working, borrowing, paying back and borrowing again. The rest were poor—lacking-bread poor.

Most of the businesses on the very long main street were Jewish, and more shops lined the side streets. We had our cobblers, tinsmiths and tailors, a great town hall and a post office.

Twice a day, the town crier went out with his drum to gather the people around him and announce the important news of the world as well as the latest happenings in town. The local gentiles, proud of Szemihaly, tried to run it like a big city. Not one of the officials of the town hall was above accepting a bribe, a fact that came in handy if one knew how to approach them.

The streets were lined with many trees, mostly acacias, and when they were in bloom they added magic to our surroundings. The trees were all over town, but the sidewalks, made of loosely spaced, unevenly cut flat stones, were not. When it rained, the mud in the unpaved side streets became so deep that one was lucky to be walking instead of sinking. Here and there a plank was laid to make passing easier, but we didn't mind walking in the mud. Our boots made swishing sounds with each step. When the mud dried, it turned into dust, and it was fun watching little puffs fly from our toes as we walked.

From the first snowfall, we could not get out of sturdy boots. The first pleasure of spring was to put on shoes; it felt like walking on air. Ditches ran between the sidewalk and the road to catch the surface water from rainfall. After a heavy downpour, the layers of dust in the small stones of the road turned into the deepest mud imaginable, and the ditches filled with water. For a few hours, we had a wonderful time wading barefoot in them. When the ditches were dry, we used to put a plank along one of their slanted sides to slide down on.

We wore out two or three pairs of shoes a year in the mud, but *Shabbos* shoes lasted long enough to pass on. Clothes were sewn at home or ordered from a dressmaker as they were needed, and there was a lot of passing down. Coats and woolen dresses that were worn out on one side were taken apart and turned inside out. By adding buttons, collars and bows, Mamuka gave them a new look.

The Szemihalyer Yeshivah was world renowned. Boys from many lands came to learn there, and since the *yeshivah* had no cooking facilities, the boys ate with families. We had different boys every day of the week, but on *Shabbos* we always had the same ones, sometimes for two seasons. The *Shabbos bachurim* were part of the family.

There was no Bais Yaakov, because the Hungarian *Chassidim* were afraid that girls might misinterpret the Torah. We attended a Jewish school under state supervision until one o'clock in the afternoon. The curriculum allowed only one hour of Jewish studies daily, and that had to include *davening*. *Chumash* was taught in Hungarian.

On occasion, I heard Mamuka express disappointment about women not being allowed to learn, but she accepted her womanhood and she was in every sense of the word a righteous woman.

The school had yearly outings. Mamuka saw to it that every child, even from the poorest family, went. Fresh rolls and ice cream were provided for rich and poor so that no child would feel uncomfortable.

We had an uncompromisingly strict and basic religious education at home. We were expected not to question why this or that had to be so; we had to accept everything because our parents said it was so, and their parents had told them it was so.

By the time I was twelve years old I already knew how to *kasher* chickens. I even knew how to split the chicken's head open and remove the tissue-thin membrane from the brain cavity.

Whenever I came home with a scraped knee from falling off a fence or out of a tree, Mamuka lovingly tended the hurt. But if I got into a scrape with one of my friends, she let me scramble out of it by myself.

"I'll tell you a little story," she would say. "Two mothers saw their children fighting. Each one picked up her own and headed home. As they walked, each claimed her child was right, and the mothers themselves almost got into a fight. Before they entered their respective homes, one of the children yelled to the other, 'I'll come out soon and we'll continue the game.'

"'Okay,' called the other.

"That's why I don't interfere," Mamuka would conclude.

I wanted to be a teacher, but that was out. I was a very poor student, and even at a very young age I understood that to be a teacher one had to be learned. Second to teaching, I wanted to be a post office "Miss," because I admired the way she used the rubber stamp. In our childhood games, I was always the post office Miss, even if I had to bribe my way into it.

Uncle Avraham Meyer opened a grocery store for his children to run, and being there with them was great fun. Once I saw a traveling salesman buy a can of sardines, open it, squeeze some lemon on it and eat if from the can. I had never tasted sardines, and lemons were expensive and not readily available. I stood there drooling until my cousin unceremoniously removed me.

Returning home, I told Mamuka, "When I'm rich, I'll buy a can of sardines and eat it all by myself."

The next time I was due for a reward, I was handed a can of sardines with a wedge of lemon, and I was given a warning to squeeze the lemon in a corner first to see if I liked it. Ironically, after dreaming about it for weeks, I did not like it with the lemon.

We were encouraged to spend time outdoors even when it was very cold, but on very hot days we were cautioned not to stay in the sun too long. One hot, sunny day, while we were playing in the store, Channah noticed that when someone walked by in the street, an upside-down reflection could be seen on the wall. It took a few days to discover that it happened only at a certain time of day. After that, a lot of friends came to see our "shadow shows." We took turns going "on stage," but I, being the youngest, was taken advantage of. I didn't mind being outside more than in; I was just as happy singing and dancing on stage as watching. We enjoyed seeing the loaded farm wagons and buggies that passed frequently and an occasional flock of geese waddling by. But the real excitement was a speeding car. The dust rose high, and before it had a chance to settle, someone was sent out to dance in what on our screen looked like the clouds.

Another form of entertainment was "music." A piece of tissue paper was draped over a comb, and we hummed as we passed our mouths back and forth over it. It sounded like the accompaniment of some instrument.

For storytelling there were tales like "Cinderella" or "Snow White and the Seven Dwarfs." I could listen for hours to my sisters talk about things they remembered from the days when Tatika was home. One story was that when Mamuka was angry, Tatika would play his violin and sing a little song of apology. This never failed to make Mamuka smile.

Mamuka always had time for us, and for anyone else who needed her. Once, when I was home sick and bored, Mamuka took a ring with a small ruby off her finger. She held it up to the light and made me look through. Fascinated by the beautiful colored light bouncing off the facets, I played happily with it for hours.

Mamuka believed that we were reading only screened material. But when we grew older, we took to reading novels that were not permitted. All our friends had them, and we exchanged, for we felt they were really harmless. Good hiding places were not easy to come by, though. When Eisik was home from *yeshivah*, he always managed to find them.

When we tired of our other games, we could always fall back on our town *nebachs*. Like any self-respecting town, we had ours. They were from good families, and the Jews took good care of them. I am ashamed to say we did tease them, in spite of repeated warnings not to.

Do-do was terrified of thunder and lightning. Black clouds sent him scuttling for cover. We used to call after him, "Do-do, the black clouds are coming." He would go into a frenzy of screaming. Mamuka forbade us to call after him, so we just pointed to the sky and got the same result.

Then there was Bumy, the official water carrier. He never talked, and no one knew whether he could speak. He had integrity. He would not accept cash, only food, and that only if he carried water first. If he was shown that the buckets were full, he took one out to the yard, carefully spilled it, and smiled. When he returned with new water in the bucket, he felt he had earned the food. He never sat down to eat, but always stood facing the wall, holding his plate. Most fascinating of all, he never stopped smiling.

We had real entertainment, too. The circus came once or twice a year, and there was a carnival with a merry-go-round as its main attraction. I couldn't get on because it made me sick, so I watched longingly as it went round and round. Looking at all the strange things was amusing enough. Once in a while, a wonderfully entertaining puppet show came. Since the entrance fee was a small amount or a few cobs of corn, everyone was able to go and then talk about it for weeks.

Mamuka had a daily and weekly newspaper coming to the house so we could keep up with world events. Radios were scarce. For a big happening, like a coronation, we all gathered at the house of the one friend who had a radio. Although the program was mostly drowned out by static, we had fun anyway.

There was also a Hungarian-language Jewish paper. Once we had a nice surprise. Without telling us, Raidl had written an article—and it was printed. The townspeople were bursting with pride.

Occasionally, films were shown in the town hall, but in our predominantly *Chassidic* town, going to the movies was frowned upon. When I was seven, talking movies came to us in the form of "Sonny Boy." This miracle one had to see. Mamuka had an idea. She rented the movie room in the town hall for an evening with the understanding that only ladies could attend. It was a huge success. Tickets were sold out in advance for two showings. Jews came from all over, and even gentile ladies and their daughters came. Ice cream and sweets were sold from my cousin's candy shop. It was an occasion to remember. For weeks I was humming the tunes from "Sonny Boy." The important thing was that the profit went to charity. Unfortunately, the event was never repeated. The *kehillah* vetoed the idea.

Every year, there were many fund-raising activities for charity, with Mamuka in the hub of it and we children always involved. Whether it was a *Purim* play at school or an afternoon tea, Mamuka was busy arranging things and helping any way she could. Her specialty was costumes, for which the fancy American dresses Tatika sent came in handy.

One day a large crate arrived marked, "Handle with care. Breakable." It was one of Tatika's delightful surprises—a phonograph with seventy-two records of the most popular *chazanim* and singers in the Yiddish world, complete with instructions in my father's careful print. It gave hours of joy to family and friends. The younger children were not allowed to touch the plates. I felt so important when it was my turn to crank that even when the others tired of doing it I was happy to continue.

Another form of entertainment was our "summer thea-ter." With our friends we made up plays, songs, dances and poetry. Then we set up chairs in the garden and invited all our neighbors. Our reward was the generous applause of an enthusiastic audience.

Chapter Nine

IN HUNGARY, PATRIOTISM WAS REQUIRED. THE ADULTS TRIED to make us actually feel patriotic so we wouldn't get into trouble by saying the wrong thing. On national holidays, the band of the junior army played in the town square, and everyone had to hang out the flag and wear red, white and green rosettes. We sang all the songs and recited the magnificent poetry about the national heroes and the battles they fought, and we really meant it when we proudly proclaimed, "I am a Hungarian." Although we knew that the gentiles did not like Jews, it was easy to forget when they smiled so sweetly. The Count, when was out in his carriage, doffed his hat even to children.

One evening, a battalion of soldiers marching from one point to another arrived in our town and encamped there. In no time at all, word spread that no Jewish girl should be out on the streets alone. Meanwhile, the town officials scuttled around to find lodgings for the officers. Since our house was big, two rooms were commandeered. Mamuka's pleas that we were all women and children fell on deaf ears.

The rooms were prepared with clean beds, water on the washstand, soap and towels. Then Mamuka proceeded to barricade the family in two other connecting rooms. She tried to act calm, but she looked quite worried. Every piece of heavy furniture that was movable was pushed against doors and windows. We hardly slept that night.

As it turned out, the officers never came back to sleep. After a night of partying, they returned early in the morning to wash up and thanked Mamuka politely before marching off.

Boys over the age of ten had to enter the junior army for compulsory after-school and weekend military training. When the junior army passed by, children stood in front of every house to watch in awe. The young boys marching in step to the music of their band made a splendid show. One Sunday, as we stood staring, we saw a Jewish boy with a broken leg, swollen eyes and bleeding nose being dragged along, supported by two others who were barely staggering, as gentile boys laughingly goaded them on. One of my friends screamed in horror, whereupon an officer stepped out of the line, came to the side of the road, and proclaimed, "That's what they get for not reporting on time!"

Anyone who could avoid enlisting did so, and Eisik was no exception. During his years in the Shopron Yeshivah, the *zsandarn* often came to our house to look for him. "He's away at school," Mamuka would tell them.

"When he comes home," the *zsandarn* warned, "he must report to the authorities."

"Certainly," Mamuka would say.

63

But of course, when he came home he did not report.

At five o'clock one morning, there was a loud banging on the door. My cousin Yankel, who was staying with us at the time, was the first one up. Although he was only twelve years old, he immediately grasped the situation and began to stall. In a sleepy voice he asked, "Who is it?" He did a lot of yawning, meanwhile hissing through the corner of his mouth, "Eisik! The *zsandarn*!" Then he asked again, "Who is it?"

Mamuka shook Eisik awake, and the entire household got up. All the while, Yankel, mumbling sleepily, fumbled with the locks. By the time he opened the door, Eisik was under his bed. Raidl, hugging herself from cold or fear, stood in her nightgown at the foot of the bed. The *zsandarn* looked into and under everything except that one bed. By then, Mamuka had a bottle with two glasses in her hand. "It's a cold morning gentlemen," she said. "Have a drink."

All smiles as they left, one of them turned to Mamuka and said, "You seem to be smarter than us. Let us know when he turns up."

Mamuka did not wait long to send Eisik back to Shopron.

Chapter Ten

EVENTUALLY, WE LOST THE USE OF THE STORE AS OUR PLAY-
room. Tatika would not come home until he had an income
to support his family. Now that all his savings had been wiped
out in the Depression, he had to start all over again from the
beginning. After long, painful months of discussion by mail,
it was decided that since the place for a store was right there
in our house, Mamuka should start a business. Since she was
very handy and artistically inclined, her first thought was in
the embroidery line. Having very little capital, she had to
borrow from family and friends. That alone was not easy for
her, accustomed as she was to giving.

The way Mamuka continued to run the house, no one
could say we were poor. Instead of hiring help, almost
everything was done by the family, except the really heavy
work. Everyone was expected to pitch in.

The beading on the fancy dresses from America was removed and sorted, and decorative pillows and pin cushions were upholstered from the fabric. In the beginning, the shelves were almost bare. But since there was no other shop like ours in town, or even in nearby towns, slowly but surely the shelves filled up not only with embroidery needs, but also with textiles.

We were all put to work. Rivkah did the design printing on a large table, which was also used for pleating. On busy days, I had to watch that people did not take anything without paying. It was boring, but I preferred it to housework.

At a time when ready-made clothes were not common in Europe, Mamuka cut aprons and simple housedresses and had a gentile woman across the street sew them. These became very popular among the farm people. Tatika suggested that cosmetics be sold, and the idea was successful. In those days a grocery or butcher store was just that and nothing else, so ours was called "the American store."

In the mornings the store was full of farm folk going to market or returning with loaded baskets on their arms. In the afternoon the wives of the professionals and officials came from far and near. Mamuka knew how to handle the farm people just as she knew the language of the elite crowd. These ladies whiled away the afternoon chatting as they fingered laces and silks. I liked to be there to watch them and listen; then I made up stories about them. There was a lot of talk about religion. Some wanted to know how we could live by those very outmoded rules. Mamuka answered, "Do you know about old wine? The older it gets, the more delectable it becomes."

When a trousseau was ordered for a bride, Mamuka hired gentile girls from our town to do the embroidery on it. The results were gratifying. After a while people began to say, "I had my daughter outfitted by Mrs. Weinstock."

Much time and energy went into organizing and running the store. It took years for the store to become profitable, and in the meantime Mamuka also raised fowl. All this was in addition to raising a large family, cooking for the *bachurim* and caring for the poor. Even when she sat down, her hands were never still. She was always working at something, making notes, writing letters or unraveling wool. She enjoyed working.

Now and then, Mamuka would go to Budapest on a shopping trip. One time, she returned in low spirits. She had tried to change a hundred dollar bill in the street, and the guy had taken off with it. A hundred dollars was a small fortune, but Mamuka couldn't call the police because it was illegal to change money in the street.

One afternoon, an official who was checking out illegal saccharine sales came into the store. Very nonchalantly, he sat on the edge of the counter and looked over to the other side, trying to see underneath. Mamuka was busy with a customer.

Young as I was, I understood that when a finance officer came into your territory it meant trouble. I was frightened, but Mamuka stayed calm.

When the customer left, Mamuka asked him, "How can I help you?"

"We had a tip that you are selling saccharine," he said.

"Who could have told them something like that?" asked Mamuka with a smile. "But as long as you are here, could you take home a small parcel that your wife bought a little earlier today?"

While she was talking, her hands were busy. She wrapped a tube of toothpaste, a brush, a small bottle of cologne and two pairs of silk stockings, and she gave the package to him.

The officer took the parcel. On his small salary, any gift came in handy.

"I don't know," he said smilingly. "Some people come up with things like this, and since there was a report, I had to check it out." At the door, he turned around one last time and asked, "Are you selling saccharine?"

"Definitely not," answered Mamuka.

After the officer left, she sat down. I saw that she was shaking.

Since Mamuka was working so hard in the store, we younger children were instructed to turn to our older sisters for help with our problems. Chayah Sarah saw to it that fresh clothes were laid out and used ones put where they belonged. I remember Chayah Sarah's soft voice telling bedtime stories while she lay next to me until I fell asleep. Raidl was charged with watching our table manners. Her voice was brusque, but her gentle hands took care of many cuts and bruises, and her arms were loving when someone needed soothing.

We had to obey our elder sisters just as they had to obey Mamuka. Although we adored Raidl, we were itching to get even with her for all the discipline she meted out. One day we got our chance. She was choking, and we banged her on the back with great relish.

Besides parents and older siblings, grandparents also were to be loved and respected. When I was born, only Tatika's mother was still alive. We lived too far from Ujhel to get to know her. One summer, Mamuka took me to see her, and I carried away a memory of a little old lady wearing a warm shawl over her shoulders despite the heat. Her dark eyes looked out at me from a shrunken little face framed by a *babushka*. We stayed only a few days, one of which was *Tishah b'Av*. My aunt forbade everyone to mention that it was a fast day in Grandmother's presence, because she would want to fast and that would not do. I was disappointed that I could not show off to her that I was still fasting.

While Tatika was working to rebuild a new future from the wreck of the Depression, letters and pictures kept coming and going. Although Mamuka did her best to keep the home front as cheerful and smooth-running as possible, my father's absence was a live wire always close to the surface, searing at our hearts and minds. We reread letters and looked at pictures, and we learned by heart the treasured poems expressing his love and longing that Tatika wrote to each of us.

Chapter Eleven

I NEVER DID LIKE SCHOOL, AND MAMUKA HAD PLENTY OF AGGRA-
vation over my schooling. I didn't study or do my homework
if I could get away with it. Whenever I could, I feigned a
stomachache or toothache.

Once when I had a bad cough, Mamuka kept me out of
school and took me along with her for a few days of shopping.
We were learning *Ashrei* at the time, and my elderly teacher
was not happy about my leaving. When I came back, she was
sure that I was not prepared, and she called on me to recite.
My wonderful mother had practiced with me daily, so I
recited the first few lines faultlessly. My teacher looked
surprised and had the grace to praise my performance. Had
she called on me again, I would have fallen flat on my face. I
knew only those first few lines.

When Mamuka finished shopping in the city, she decided

to visit her niece Raizy in Apagy, a town so small it probably wasn't on the map. We arrived in the afternoon to screams of anguish. Raizy's youngest child, a little girl, died of an illness just as we arrived. There was no way to let the family know in time to get to the funeral, so it was through Hashem's providence that we came when we did. Mamuka, who thought I was too young to witness the tragedy, was upset that I was there, but I helped by playing with Raizy's two little boys while the adults took care of the necessary arrangements.

Upon leaving Apagy, we headed for Mamuka's cousin Fanny and her family on an estate in Gesthely. When we got off the train, it was almost dark. Mamuka had no choice but to hire a buggy to take us out to the estate, but she was nervous about making the trip in the dark. The hired driver was a jolly fellow. "Don't worry," he said. "I'll get you there safely."

We were hardly on the way when he stopped at an inn with a promise to come out soon. Mamuka did not reply. But when he stopped soon after at a second inn, she pleaded with him to stop. "Enough!" said Mamuka. "You're already drunk."

"Don't worry," he said again.

By then it was dark, and I was shivering, not so much from cold as from sensing Mamuka's fear.

At last, we arrived. The cousins were surprised and happy to see us, and we spent a thoroughly enjoyable weekend with them.

Chapter Twelve

ONE OF MY TEACHERS WAS ALWAYS AFTER ME. "IF YOU WANTED to," he would say, "you could do better at school."

I knew he would not punish me because he felt sorry for me, and I played on his sympathy. He sometimes asked me if I ate enough, because I was so skinny. Once, when he pinched my cheek, he noticed that my face was fuller than usual.

"Tell your mother to take you to the doctor," he instructed me. "Your face is swollen."

When I told Mamuka, she laughed and said, "It's time to start a diet."

Overnight, I had become quite plump.

The word "diet" was not new to me. In our town almost all the mothers were overweight. Matronly, it was called. They were always talking about starting a diet tomorrow. The standards for acceptable weight, though, were different from those of today. Chayah Sarah, who was tall, slim and beautiful, was thought skinny. After her first baby was born, she remained with fifteen extra pounds, and people said, "Now she could enter a beauty contest."

In spite of all the ovens in the house, not all the rooms were heated all the time. Our bedroom was cold. In frigid weather, we got undressed in the living room, where a big fire was always burning, and made a run for our beds through the cold, giggling and screaming with pleasure as we slid between the icy sheets. We were a hardy bunch, seldom ill.

For us children, strep throats, chicken pox, measles and mumps were fun. We were almost never alone, because at least two of us would catch the same illness. We felt special and pampered. I used to feel sorry when it was over and I had to go back to school.

Real sickness was different. Feige contracted typhus. That was when "Esther" was added to her name.

The house was hushed; no one sang or even spoke loudly. Feige needed twenty-four-hour care. Mamuka and Raidl took turns staying up at night, and the rest of us sat with her during the day, with instructions to call if we needed help. Mamuka came often to check. Just when Feige was feeling better, she suffered a relapse. Large sheets were dampened and wrapped around her to bring down the high fever. When Feige was at all lucid she asked for Raidl; she was more willing to take a sip of water or a spoonful of soup from Raidl than from her mother. Raidl, who fulfilled her duties lovingly, was on the brink of exhaustion.

One day, I walked into a room which I thought was unoccupied. The room was in semi-darkness, and I felt more than saw that someone was there. When my eyes adjusted to the dimness, I saw that it was Mamuka. With her arms stretched toward heaven, she beseeched Hashem not to take this precious child He had given into her keeping.

I did not tell anyone, because once when I saw her *daven Minchah*, she asked me not to tell anyone outside our household. As a rule, women did not *daven* on weekdays, except to say the morning *berachos*. We were never urged to *daven* on weekdays, but on *Shabbos*, *davening* was a must. Nevertheless, it was not my favorite pastime, and if I could I tried to get away without doing it. At times, though, I had a yearning to *daven*, and it bothered me that I did not do it regularly. When I voiced my feelings to Mamuka, she said, "To me, wanting to *daven* came later in life." I took this as encouragement rather than reprimand.

One day, Feige opened her eyes, and out of the blue, she announced, "I feel better."

At first, there was disbelief, then cautious jubilation. The news travelled fast, and we all wanted to see and hear. We were allowed to visit her one by one for a short time.

For a while, she was not allowed much food. When the doctor said she could have some solids, she asked for chicken. The doctor forbade that, but allowed a small amount of well-cooked pigeon. This excited her. But Mamuka was afraid to feed her anything except strong soups and farina. She thought Feige would forget by the next day.

Feige didn't forget, so an elaborate plan was worked out. She was to be told that the pigeon was ready to be taken to the *shochet*. At a given time, the maid was supposed to yell, "*Oy!* The pigeon got away!" Someone closer to the room was to take up the cry and repeat it.

Not to be left out, I stood closest to her room and cried out, "The maid let the silly pigeon go!"

Mamuka was in the room in case Feige needed consoling. My sister's face registered disappointment, but she said, "Oh, I don't like pigeon anyway."

74

Feige's convalescence was very slow and painful to watch. First, she would sit on the side of the bed, her feet dangling. Then she graduated to a chair for short periods of time. She had been a beautiful child, but now she was skinny as a rail and bald. When a few sparse hairs started to grow, to our horror Mamuka shaved it off to make it grow in more thickly. Her hair grew back, a halo of dense chestnut curls.

At about that time, there was an influx of Russian girls to do housework, and the entire town became infested with lice. No one knew what to do about it; none of the strong solutions helped. When Mamuka shaved Feige's head, she did the same for us younger children. We were not happy about it, but it worked! We grew thick, beautiful lice-free hair. As shocked as the town was, after a while they followed suit.

Chapter Thirteen

EVERYTHING AROUND THE HOME WAS HARD WORK. FORTU-
nately, the peasants worked for pennies, especially after the
harvest.

We always had a girl-of-all-work staying in the little room
off the kitchen. At some point in my childhood we had a
Russian woman named Anna. When the snow was very deep
or it was raining hard, Anna carried me to school on her
strong back. She never found it too difficult to do something
extra for me.

Anna had a little girl younger than me, and in spite of all
she did for me, I was still jealous of the child. One day, when
she was waiting near the cellar door for her mother to come
up, I gave her a push hard enough to send her rolling down
the few steps. She screamed, and Anna started yelling in
Russian and broken Hungarian. I was a little frightened,

because I realized that I should not have done it. The commotion was loud enough to bring everyone from whatever they were doing.

Mamuka was very angry. "Giteleh," she said. "How could you do something like that to a small child?"

She raised her hand to slap me. I shrunk back. Anna rushed to my defense. In one motion, she slid her child to the ground and hugged me, so the slap meant for me landed on her. Everyone thought that was very funny, but I felt guilty and ran off crying.

I was awed by the fact that even though she was very angry at me, Mamuka still called me Giteleh, the affectionate form of Gitel. All through the years, no matter what cause I gave her to be angry, I was always Giteleh. Mamuka always claimed that she loved all her children equally, because "I have only has one Chayah Saraleh, one Raidleh, one Feigeleh . . ."

When we were mischievous, Mamuka would say, "I love you, but I don't like you."

Because she loved us, Mamuka made sure we were prepared for the rigors of life by giving all of us chores in the store and the house.

At a very early age, I had to learn to hold a needle. I remember embroidering one doily with one hundred and sixty variously sized dots in shades of lilac. I thought I'd lose my mind over it, but Mamuka would not let me stop. "There is no such thing as 'I can't' or 'I don't know how,'" she said. "If you really want to do it, and you try hard enough, you can do anything." Following Mamuka's lesson, there was never a task I hesitated to undertake.

There were times, though, when I felt I was not properly appreciated. Once while Mamuka was away for a few days, I decided to surprise her by cleaning one of the spice racks on the kitchen wall. When it shone, I hung a sign on it:

The nicest reward to get for this
Is my dearest mother's kiss.

I called her attention to it as soon as possible. After properly admiring it, she gave me a kiss and a rejoinder. "Very nice, but why didn't you do the other one, too?"

Instead of developing a hang-up for the rest of my life, I tried just a little harder the next time.

On washing day, I was put to ironing small pieces. The iron, full of hot coals, was heavier than me.

I remember laundry day in the summer, when the clothes were drying in the fragrant sunny air. My arm was up to the elbow in the deliciously cold water, and the sky was as blue as the color I was mixing into the rinse water.

In the winter, the kitchen was steamy and warm from the many pots of water put up to boil for the washing.

Once I got curious about the little pot with the white stones soaking in it. Not knowing it was washing soda, I tasted it. My screams were heard by the neighbors.

One evening, when the washing was done, the maid was polishing the stove. Having heard that sugar would make it shine, she put some into the cleansing mixture just when a neighbor's son came by. One day, he licked the hot stove to see if it was sweet. He went around with his tongue hanging out for days.

For years a thief went around on washing nights, silently removing the clothes from the attics where they were hung to dry. The Fleet-Footed Fox, as we called him, didn't stop at clean linens. A lot of *Pesach* dishes that were stored in the attics disappeared as well—a tragic loss for some. He was finally caught in a grocery store, but none of the things he took were ever recovered.

As we got older, we were assigned chores that were not

liked, such as washing dishes in two extra large bowls, one filled with hot water, the other with cold for rinsing. Although most of the time there were peasant girls to help with the housework, *kashering* chickens and meat always had to be done by members of the family. In the winter it was unbelievably hard. Salting was done in the kitchen, but rinsing had to be done outdoors by the well. The ice-cold water made the hands numb and red as the blood on the meat.

Work of one form or another was always going on in the vegetable and flower gardens. Spring brought the smell of fresh earth being spaded and turned over by hired peasant men. Mamuka would stoop down with them to plant and weed, and we children were encouraged to join in, too. Every year or two, fresh pebbles were put down on the walks among the beds. I can still sense the rich sunshine on the growing things.

Our neighbor Mrs. Bodek had a beautiful, well-tended garden. For hours she would work there, stooping down to weed and plant. I watched for the fruit on her trees to grow big and ripe. Then, while she was inside, I climbed the trees and filled my pockets. Afterwards, when I saw her looking up at the tree, my heart pounded with fear and guilt. I was sure she was counting the fruits to see how many were missing.

As soon as the weather turned warm enough, the gentile girls Mamuka hired to do embroidery for the store would ply their needles in the garden. When it rained, they used the veranda. That's where we *davened* on *Shabbos* mornings in the summer, after waking up to the music of Eisik's voice reviewing the *Sedra* with his friend Muttel Bodek. Although he did it in the winter, too, it sounded even sweeter through the clear warm air.

On winter nights, before a cozy fire, the hired girls would sing as their fingers busily selected and pulled goose down.

79

One of the girls would make fluffy popcorn on the open fire for everyone.

Thursday was baking day. Those who did not have ovens prepared their breads and cakes at home and then brought them to the baker. People came from all directions carrying bread baskets and baking pans of all sizes and shapes. We only had to go next door, where our widowed neighbor supplemented her earnings as a seamstress by heating her oven on Thursdays. In the summer, when we had no fire going, our *cholent* was put into her oven along with all the others. Picking up the *cholent* on *Shabbos* was almost a social event among the gentile maids, who were always accompanied by a member of the family. If you didn't have a maid, the neighbor's maid was more than happy to pick up your *cholent,* too.

On Thursdays in the winter, our big oven was put to use. Big round crusty breads and all kinds of cakes poured out of it. After they cooled, Mamuka cut, sliced, packed and sent us all over delivering to the homes of the poor.

Sometimes when I open a can of tomato juice, I remember the endless work that went into making it at home. A big iron urn stood on an open fire in the kitchen yard. Bottles and jars had to be washed with long-handled brushes, coarse salt and rice. Then they had to be sterilized. Finally, the cooked tomatoes had to be strained. Someone always checked that the jars were shiny enough and that every drop of juice was extracted from the tomatoes.

The filled bottles and jars were placed in baking pans filled with water and covered with wet towels. Then, with a prayer and a promise of *tzedakah,* they were put in the large oven that was preheated to supposedly the right temperature so none of the jars would crack. Inevitably, some did. Besides the loss, it made a colossal mess.

It was immensely satisfying to see those bottles and jars

lined up on the pantry shelves, again with the hope that none would spoil. But of course, some did. They had to be checked periodically, and the ones that showed any sign of aging were used up first. The question came up, "When will the good ones be eaten? When they start spoiling?"

The whole procedure of preserving was very boring, but we found ways of alleviating the boredom. When plums, cherries and peaches were pitted for jams and preserves, we saved the pits. At the end of the afternoon, when we knew it was time for the herd of pigs to pass through town, we spread the pits in a thick layer across the road (never in front of our house). Then we hid behind fences and bushes and watched the herdsmen curse and ply their whips to urge the animals on, but to no avail. The pigs did not budge as long as there was one pit left to crack.

One summer, the boredom of bottle washing was broken by one of the cats giving birth to kittens in the woodshed just beyond the summer kitchen. We did more watching than washing.

Chapter Fourteen

BY 1935, BUSINESS WAS GOING WELL, AND SO WERE TATIKA'S savings. He felt secure enough financially to come home, but the threat of Hitler worried him. He decided to apply for first papers, a prerequisite for citizenship, so that he would be able to re-enter the United States and bring his family if necessary. His admission that he had been in America illegally for eleven years caused a two-year delay in the issuance of the papers.

In the meantime, he sent home money for Chayah Sarah's wedding and dowry. The necessary linens were prepared in our business. Peasant girls, who worked for pennies, were hired to do the sewing and embroidery.

There were gentile customers with whom we were on friendly terms. One of them was the head gardener on the baronial estate—no small title. These fine, quiet people used to send us baskets of fruit and vegetables in season. They had one son and one daughter. The young man, who was always faultlessly polite, used to walk the long distance to our home with offerings of the first ripe cherries. On Chayah Sarah's wedding day, they sent a wagonload of every type of flower that was in bloom in their hothouses.

Before the wedding, Mamuka told Chayah Sarah, "Remember, my child. Hashem comes first always, then your husband. After that, Father and Mother."

A year later, Chayah Sarah's father-in-law put her dowry money into a bank account on Raidl's name and mailed the bankbook to Mamuka with a letter saying, "A person like my daughter-in-law does not need a dowry."

Moments like that made life worth living in spite of all the hardships.

After the son of the head gardener went to university in one of the large cities, we did not see the family for a while. One sunny Sunday, Mamuka and I were taking a walk, and she decided to visit them. The young man, who had returned home, was wearing a black shirt with arrows on the collar. He did not greet us, and the others were noticeably ill at ease. We left as soon as decently possible. A few days later, the daughter came to buy something in our store. After greetings were exchanged, she burst into tears and told Mamuka that her brother forbade them to go into a Jewish store or to have anything to do with Jews. "If he finds out that I came into your store," she said, "he will harm me."

We had always known of anti-Semitism, but this was the first time we came so brutally close to it.

We came closer yet. The boys in town began to taunt the Jews by calling out, *"Heil Hitler!"* Rocks were thrown at Jewish windows.

One day, Mamuka asked me to take some urgent sewing to the gentile woman across the street. I wanted to stay and play with her daughter, but when the woman took the package from me at the door, I realized she did not me want me to enter because her husband was drunk. I was not afraid; I knew he was harmless. While the girl and I played in the yard, he staggered out and watched us. I didn't pay attention to his rambling until I heard, "When Hitler comes in, I'll take the Weinstock house."

As I dropped the toy and started running home in fright, I heard the girl crying and calling to her mother. That was the last time I was allowed to visit there; any more playing had to be done on our grounds. Although Mamuka told me not to worry about the incident, I could not get it out of my mind.

Rumors of war reached our town, and preparations were made for blackout training in case the town was bombed. The civil defense was in the hands of coarse, uneducated gentiles. Jewish boys were drafted, and Jewish girls were expected to volunteer. Carried away by patriotism, some girls did join, and the stories that were whispered could freeze a Jewish mother's heart.

The *frum* parents worried about their children getting ruined. When rumors spread that girls would be drafted, Mamuka was approached to find out what the truth was. This was not a simple matter; Mamuka's diplomacy no longer accomplished what it used to. The lady on the other side of the fence was afraid to come when Mamuka called her, and it was getting harder and harder to bribe officials. Nevertheless, Mamuka tried anyway, and she came back with the answer that girls were not likely to be drafted. Although no official's word meant anything anymore, it gave our people some hope.

Rich Jews began to send large amounts of cash out of the country "for the future." At the same time, travelling to neighboring cities to collect funds became harder. It grew increasingly difficult to marry off poor girls, and a few in our town were left old maids. At a time when Hungarian Jews were beginning to flee, there were families who had the papers to leave Hungary but no money for the trip. Mamuka argued endlessly with some of her affluent friends to help those people save themselves, but to no avail. Ultimately, much of the money deposited in Swiss bank accounts was never reclaimed.

Chapter Fifteen

MEALTIME WAS TOGETHERNESS TIME. MAMUKA WANTED US TO
speak Yiddish at the table because there was not much chance
to do so any other time. We were not encouraged to use
Yiddish in the street, because the gentiles did not approve. In
school, Hungarian was the compulsory language. In the
store, Yiddish might be an insult to customers. As a result,
our Yiddish was very limited. At the table, we ended up using
a comic mixture of Yiddish and Hungarian. There was so
much laughter that we could hardly wait for mealtime.

One evening in 1937, right after dinner, Mamuka took a
"very important" letter out of her pocket. The letter rattled
in her hand. As she read it aloud, I went into a sort of trance.
The only thing I heard was one sentence: "I have booked
passage home on the *Queen Mary*."

I did not wait to hear the date of arrival. Before anyone

could stop me, I was out the door, and in five minutes, the entire town knew that Tatika was coming home. I saw gladness in people's faces, but also doubt. The overall feeling was, "We shall see."

On my way home, I sat down on a stone in the street to think. The enormity of the words "father is coming home" hit me full force. I wanted to take the town crier's drum and stop at every corner to announce my wonderful news just in case someone had not heard. I did not want to think about the doubt I saw on people's faces.

The family plunged into feverish preparations. The house, never dirty, was gone over from cellar to attic as for *Pesach*. After all, Tatika's money had built the house. We were proud of it, and we wanted him to see it at an advantage.

Mamuka went around in a daze. Raidl organized the work crew, consisting of us younger children, the maid and the washerwoman from town.

I was just about finished applying some gooey polish to the legs of the large dining room table, when I heard the tinkling of a bicycle bell. Carefully, I put the rag on top of the polish bottle; then I ran to see who in the neighborhood was getting a telegram. To my amazement, the telegram delivery man stopped in front of our house and carefully propped his bicycle against the wall. By then a large group of children had gathered. Mamuka came to the door and took the envelope handed to her. With a sinking feeling in my heart I followed Mamuka into the store, which was empty at the moment. As she read it, her knees buckled, and she sank into the nearest chair. By this time, the rest of the family had come through an inside door. Everyone held his breath as she read the short message aloud, "Due to minor fire on board, the *Queen Mary* will not sail as scheduled."

Someone was entering from the street. Mamuka pulled

herself together. Business had to be conducted as usual. Raidl, putting on a sergeant's demeanor to mask her pain, ordered everyone back to their tasks.

As I continued to apply polish to the table leg as if there was nothing more important in the world, my tears kept falling. I was not crying for myself. My life was carefree enough, with nothing really missing. I was crying for Mamuka. I knew there was a lot of affection between my parents that all the time of separation had not dulled. Thirteen years out of their beautiful young lives. Thirteen years alone, caring for seven children and not cringing from any kind of labor to bring him home sooner. Thirteen years of yearning.

We were always taught not to ask questions about life's misfortunes, but the question was there: Why?

I felt like my heart was breaking. As I sat there sniveling, I did not notice that my tears were streaking the fresh polish. All of a sudden, Raidl's voice behind me snapped, "Look what you're doing!"

I looked and saw the ugly streaks my tears had left on the fresh polish. Without stopping to think that she, too, was upset by the telegram, I threw the damp rag on the floor and bolted from the room. I ran to my friend Jolan's house and blurted out to her, "My father was delayed. He's not coming home this week."

Jolan's mother, sitting nearby, whispered to her sister-in-law, "I don't think he will ever come home."

I ran out of there like a beaten puppy and kept running until I reached the woodshed in our backyard. I sat down on a pile of wood to cry and brood. After a while, the pity for Mamuka eased a little. I felt annoyed that no one came looking for me, and besides, I was hungry, so I went to see how the rest of the family was doing .

If I expected hysterics, there were none. It was dinner

time, and everything looked normal. The two *yeshivah* boys who ate with us, as well as our family, were sitting at their usual places. Mamuka, with a slight redness around the eyes, was ladling soup at the head of the table as usual.

I don't know how she went on during the next days and weeks. There was no further communication from Tatika. Not knowing what was happening with him was even worse than the certainty of not having him home. Living through those days with the words of Jolan's mother ringing in my ears, I became very subdued. No one noticed. Everyone was busy with his own misery.

As long as those days seemed, they also passed. Responsibilities, home, children, business, and the constant helping of others kept Mamuka busy—and always watching for the mailman.

Then another telegram arrived, and we came running from all over. Mamuka opened the envelope and read the message. A trembling smile broke through, mingled with tears. Her face looked like the sun-filled sky after a summer rain.

AM IN BUDAPEST. WILL BE ARRIVING AT TOWN DEPOT TOMORROW.

I was on the run again, but this time Mamuka was quicker than me. She grabbed my arm and stopped my flight. The surprise on my face as I turned made everyone laugh. It was the first time in weeks there was real laughter in the house. "No one is to know," said Mamuka, "until Tatika is actually in the house."

If we had dared to talk about it, we would surely have discovered some doubt in all our hearts. But I did not want to talk about it. I wanted to believe that the magic of expectation was real. This time there was no organized cleaning, not even special cooking or baking, just a feeling of being someplace outside, looking in.

There were a lot of volunteers eagerly offering to go to the station. I imagined myself proudly sitting beside Tatika in the carriage for all to see. But none of us were going. Mamuka arranged for Uncle to go meet him at arrival time.

The store entrance was closed. We were all gathered in the large living room, a few steps up from the store. Mamuka had closed the shutters, so that in the semi-darkness we would not see her face. I didn't like it. I wanted to hang out the window to be the first to see Tatika. But in those days, parents decided and children did.

There was absolute silence in the room. One could feel the tension. Suddenly, we heard the faint clip-clop of horses' hooves coming closer. In that breathless moment, I thought, "It will pass by." But no. The carriage stopped in front of our house. We were fixed in our places like statues. The door opened, and in walked the handsomest man I had ever seen. Although the room was charged with emotion, there was order. Everyone was recognized and greeted in turn.

I should have acted more like an adult, but the pain and humiliation of the past weeks got the better of me. Before Tatika had been in the room for fifteen minutes, I tugged at Mamuka's sleeve. She looked at me and nodded.

I ran straight to Jolan's house. Her mother answered the door. Without even greeting her I blurted out, "My father is home."

I did not wait for an answer. The shock on her face was enough for me, and I chuckled all the way home. I wanted to get back fast to make sure he was really there and to see what he had brought me, but people kept stopping me to ask about Tatika's return. Their hugs and smiling faces are still with me.

There were wonderful presents for all of us, but the most precious one I found when, without permission, I looked into one of his suitcases—letters that we wrote to him while he was in America. Among the things he saved were the pressed flowers tied with colorful little bows that we had sent as an offering of love.

Chapter Sixteen

WHO WOULD DO THE MOST FOR TATIKA TURNED INTO A CONTEST.
Since I had always been able to cheer Mamuka by singing, I
tried that. He enjoyed it. The first few times, he had tears in
his eyes.

During the years in America he had been preparing his
own meals and had eaten very simply. Other than the tins of
fowl liver conserved in *schmaltz* that Mamuka would occasionally send him, Tatika had not eaten meat all those years. Now
that he was home, Mamuka outdid herself cooking for him.
The sudden change in diet did not agree with him, but he
continued to eat so that her feelings would not be hurt.

One day, Tatika had a fainting spell. I was sent running
for Doctor Kabay, a fine gentile. On the way, I tripped and
took a rolling dive into a ditch. Despite the pain in my knee,
I immediately got up and continued running.

The doctor and I rode to our home in his buggy. After examining Tatika and asking a few questions, he prescribed bicarbonate of soda and advised eating lightly for a few days.

A week or so later, when the scare about Tatika had blown over, he noticed that I was limping.

"It's nothing," I said.

At his insistence I showed him my knee, and he nearly fainted again. This time, he took me to the doctor.

My wound was properly cleaned and bandaged. While I was sitting and recuperating from the ordeal, Tatika and Doctor Kabay conversed.

Part of the talk was about Hitler and the uproar he had caused, especially among the students.

"You picked the wrong time to come home," said the doctor. "It is clear that the Hungarian people will collaborate with the Nazis. If you can, go back and take the family with you."

The words "go back" startled me. "Tatika," I asked, as we walked home hand in hand, "are you really planning to go back to America?"

"If I go back," he reassured me optimistically, "I will bring the family."

That one year he was home was not perfect. Life still had its ups and downs. But Tatika was not a picture or a letter anymore. No one asked "Would he like this?" or "If he were here . . .?" He was here on *Pesach*, at the head of the table, and Uncle came from *shul* to wish us a "*Gut Yom Tov*" before going home to make his *Seder*, this time without us. Tatika was here on *Sukkos*, and he saw, and not always, but mostly, he approved.

Chayah Sarah came home with her baby Shayaleh as often as she could, and Eisik came home from *yeshivah* to visit. Tatika enjoyed all the wonders of family life that he had missed for so many years. It was as it should be. Raidl even dared to ask Tatika, "What reason was good enough to keep you away from the family for so long?" But of course, she did not remember the years when there was practically no bread in the house.

It was so blissful having my father home that I did not notice the whispered talk in the house about Tatika going back. No one wanted to admit that his homecoming was just for a year. He had brought home some sophisticated tools of his trade, with the thought of working in a corner of the store. But the rise of anti-Semitism made him change his plans. The final decision was made after he saw a stone thrown at someone and heard the yell "Dirty Jew!" Then and there he decided to bring the family to America.

Tatika learned that Chayah Sarah, Raidl and Eisik would have to be left behind. Eisik and Chayah Sarah's husband could not get out of Hungary because they were of military age. Moreover, immigration to America was restricted. Even if Chayah Sarah were willing to leave her husband, she and Raidl would have to wait years to enter America under the regular quota. Feige, Channah, Rivkah and I would be able to enter quickly on a special quota for children under eighteen. But Tatika would have to work fast; Feige was already seventeen. He would have to go to America in order to send us the appropriate papers.

I no longer worried what the neighbors would say when he went away. I had finally met my father and learned to trust him. But I did not want to believe it was really happening. We wanted Tatika to stay home, the place where we were born and raised, and where we belonged. But it was out of the question. Hungarian Jews were leaving their homes, some heading for Palestine, most for America. The ones who stayed were those who had papers but no money and those who had money but couldn't get papers. There were also those who recalled other uprisings which people had survived without leaving the country of their birth, and they did not want to believe that this uprising would be worse. Everyone, though, was of the opinion that we were lucky to have the opportunity to go.

Throughout his stay at home, Tatika took every chance to talk about the wonders of America. It was not necessary to light a fire in the stove to heat the apartment; there was central heating. Instead of starting a fire for cooking with kindling wood, you just turned a knob, and there was gas to cook with. We had to get drinking water from a town pump, and if we wanted it cold, a pitcher was tied to a piece of rope and lowered into the well in our yard. Vegetables were stored in sand in the cellar. Fruit was lowered into the well in a basket to cool. Who could imagine getting cold water from a tap or a refrigerator day or night, or eating fresh fruit and vegetables even in wintertime? I dreamed of America, from where all our goodies came. But we had lots of goodies already, so why couldn't we just stay home and enjoy?

Yet my heart told me there were hard times ahead. And I worried about Mamuka. How would she be able to take still more separations, from Tatika, from Feige and Channah, and finally, from Chayah Sarah and Shayeleh, Raidl and Eisik?

Chapter Seventeen

AFTER TATIKA LEFT, THE EMPTINESS WAS INDESCRIBABLE. IT seemed like an eternity until the first letter came, full of love, hope, and promise. In a shorter time than seemed possible, papers came for Feige and Channah, and preparations were made for their departure.

Oceans of tears went into those preparations. Letting her two precious children undertake a major journey in such turbulent times was almost unbearable. Then and many times afterwards, I heard Mamuka say, "May we not be tried with as much pain as we can bear."

Even though Tatika had remained a good Jew, there was plenty to worry about. Everyone knew that the *"goldene land"* did not breed true *Yiddishkeit*. Uncle had suggested that Mamuka go first to size up the situation, but Tatika was opposed. "If we wait too long," he wrote, "it will be too late for them to get in on the special quota, and on a regular one they might, Heaven forbid, never make it. I have to think with my head, not with my heart. If I had dared to go after my heart, I would have given up what I worked for all those years and stayed home with all of you."

Mamuka tried to put her soul into her children in those last few weeks. "Don't forget your home. Remember your upbringing at all times. Please don't forget to write, and above all, don't forget that you are a *Yiddishe tochter. Modeh Ani* in the morning, *Shema* at night before you go to sleep, and always remember Hashem."

Eisik also spoke to his sisters, again being a little extreme to impress his point. "It's better not to live than to live without what you have learned to believe in, because that is the only true way to live."

In the meantime, Raidl became engaged. With Feige and Channah leaving soon after the wedding, there was a lot to do. Chayah Sarah came home "to help." That was the joke of the household. Coming from a tiny town, she wanted to take advantage of the services available in Szemihaly, but she was so busy with Shayaleh that we had to do it all for her. She dispatched one of us youngsters to the cobbler, another to the pharmacy or dressmaker. We didn't mind; helping her was a pleasure.

Shayaleh, who was a very smart little boy, didn't want to eat the spinach that my sister tried to feed him because the doctor said it was healthy. Once, when he did eat it, she came running to tell Mamuka that little Shayaleh must be sick; he did not know what he was doing. In those days, that baby was the only one for whom Mamuka could produce a genuine smile.

Mamuka's sister Aunt Gitel came a week before the wedding to help. Then relatives and friends from out of town began to come. All our neighbors' empty beds were occupied by our guests.

I helped Aunt Gitel strip chicken feet. She was a good teacher of the art. I had never seen so many of them at once, but by the time we were finished, I could almost do it with my eyes closed. Every part of the chicken was utilized so as not to waste anything.

There were so many fish, I couldn't imagine who was going to eat them all. But the main attraction was the slaughtering of a calf right in our yard. All the boys in town became slaughterers that afternoon, demonstrating with sticks how it was done.

We had one guest whose parents were in America, and she was also scheduled to go. She showed me something her mother had sent her. It looked like a wide rubber tube, and she said it was a girdle. When she put it on I saw it was very practical, and since I had gained more weight than I cared for, I was very interested in the piece.

The wedding was a great success. Unfortunately, the marriage was not. Mamuka, whose outlook on life was as enlightened as her manner of dress was old-fashioned, did not insist that Raidl stick it out. Although she did not like the idea of divorce, the thought of it was not taboo. "Why should two people be unhappy for a lifetime?" said Mamuka. "If they divorce and remarry, four could be happy."

On departure day, Feige and Channah had a treat. A salesman arrived in a car, and since Mamuka was very busy, he offered to drive her and my sisters to the station in his car in exchange for a few minutes of her time during which he would describe his wares to her. While the car was being loaded, some children stood around admiring it. After all, it wasn't every day a car arrived.

Although good-byes had already been said, friends and

neighbors were there to wave farewell. As soon as the car started rolling, the dust behind it was so dense it was impossible to see, but we, a small family now, remained standing there, hoping to see them once more after the dust settled.

Chayah Sarah and her baby stayed with us until Mamuka returned from Budapest, where she had watched her children board the train that took them away from her. I had the awful feeling Mamuka would never smile again. She later wrote, "I wanted to pull back that great iron monster that was speeding away with part of my heart."

A week later, we were notified that at four o'clock that afternoon we would receive a phone call at the post office. I could hardly keep up with Mamuka as we ran there. There was a wonderful feeling of *"Baruch Hashem,* they arrived safely." Speaking to Tatika, however briefly, did Mamuka a world of good. I was disappointed, though, that I didn't get to speak on the phone.

Before returning to *yeshivah,* Eisik spoke to Mamuka about getting married. It was understood by both sides that eventually Tatika's shy, pretty niece would become his wife. Years before, after stopping off in Ujhel for a few days on his way home from *yeshivah,* he had told Mamuka, "I want to marry Rifkeleh."

"How do you know?" Mamuka had asked. "Did you have a conversation with her?"

"No," replied Eisik, "but I observed her *eidelkeit* at the table, and I know that this is it."

Mamuka smiled at her sixteen-year old son. "When the time comes," she said, "we'll talk about it."

Subsequently, Mamuka had mentioned it to the family and learned that Rifkeleh was waiting for Eisik.

Now the time had come, but Mamuka did not want Eisik married until she herself was in America and had tried everything to get him out of Hungary. No one knew how she planned to do it, but good son that he was, he obeyed.

The letters that finally came from Feige and Channah were full of excitement about the trip and about America. They missed us terribly and could hardly wait for our arrival.

That also came. We were due to leave on March 15, 1939, the day after *Purim*.

Chapter Eighteen

ONE OF THE FAMILIES IN OUR TOWN WANTED RIVKAH TO STAY home and marry their son. Mamuka wrote to ask Tatika what to do. His answer was a definite no. "If Rivkah stays home," he wrote, "you should also." That's how strongly he felt about getting us all to America before the real trouble began.

Mamuka had new outfits made for Rivkah and me, identical except for small variations in style. Rivkah was slim and I was not, so mine had a straighter line. When we went for fittings, Mamuka was careful about every small detail. Despite all the things she had to take care of, Mamuka put a lot of time into the selection of our new clothes. Pastel batistes of the finest quality were made into underwear for us, embroidered and initialed. At the same time, Mamuka put together a complete trousseau for Feige, for she was of marriageable age. The trousseau was packed very carefully, together with a decorative headboard pillow designed and made by Mamuka.

A few weeks after it was mailed, we received a letter saying that the crate had been opened at the border, and since it was against the law (it was not made clear which law) to transport the intercepted goods, they would be donated to the Horthy Action, a charity for Hungarian soldiers. "Thank you very much, in the name of Miklos Horthy."

There was no protesting this injustice. Miklos Horthy was the absolute ruler of Hungary. In school we avoided mentioning his name, because leaving out his long string of titles evoked a reprimand.

Mamuka wanted us to visit her parents' graves in Mad before we left. It was a long, tiring journey. On the way, we stopped at the house of the Kereztur Rebbe. Mamuka discussed her hesitations about going to America. He told her to go.

"*Rebbe!*" cried Mamuka. "What will happen to my other children?"

The *Rebbe* did not answer for what seemed like a long time. Then, very quietly, he said, "You must go as planned."

He gave us a *berachah*, and we left.

Mamuka's birthplace was a town much smaller than ours, and the house in which she grew up was tiny. The three rooms were still furnished with the same furniture as when Mamuka lived there. Everything was very old but spotlessly clean and neat. Mamuka showed us the little window where Zeidy used to do business and the place where a little table and a chair used to stand so he could learn between customers.

In the house lived Mamuka's brother-in-law, a widower, with his family. The children we knew well because they spent a lot of time with us. It was their Yankeleh who had stalled the *zsandarn* when they came looking for Eisik. They welcomed us very graciously. After refreshments, one of the girls came with us to the cemetery. It was painful to see Mamuka at the grave of her parents and sister. It seemed so final, that farewell.

The brightest spot on that trip was our visit to Chayah Sarah, who lived with her in-laws. I can still remember the warmth of that welcome. After a few days, we went back home. In spite of everyone's attempts at lightness, there was a certain gloom. Even spring seemed late in coming.

The time had come to decide what to do with our possessions. The store was emptied out, but there was no one to watch upside down "shadow shows." Mamuka sold what she could and gave the rest away. Our home, however, was full of a lifetime of memories. The question "Should we take this?" arose constantly. In the end, Mamuka decided not to empty the house of any furnishings, not even the china or cutlery. She did not want Raidl and Eisik, who would be living there, to feel that the house had been stripped. We packed almost nothing except our clothes. We were going forward to a new life taking only ourselves.

Mamuka had a final long talk with Uncle. Over and over again, she told him, "Don't worry. I'll make America *frum.*"

"Don't try to make America over," said Uncle. "Just be careful not to let America make you over."

By the time *Purim* arrived, everything was packed and ready. A *Purim* feast was prepared, and with the arrival of evening the house was bursting with people. Those who couldn't get in waited for others to leave so they could enter. There was plenty of food, my cousin made merry music on his violin, and the men sang along. There was no thought of our five o'clock in the morning departure time.

We became aware of it when we heard the two buggies arrive. It was prearranged that no one was going with us to the depot. Mamuka felt it would be easier that way. Also, the fact that a lot of people were there made the heart-wrenching farewell less personal. In spite of the early hour, more people came out of their houses. I heard one woman remark to another, "She'll be missed in more ways than one. Who will take care of the poor?"

My last glimpse is fixed forever in my mind. A few paces in front of the large crowd stood Chayah Sarah holding Shayeleh, with her husband at her side, Raidl, who was separated from her husband, and Eisik—a forlorn little group. It was too dark yet to see tears, if there were any. Everyone waved and cheered. Then, as the horses took off, a deep silence fell. As I looked back, I saw Mamuka turn around once. We did not speak. As we got farther and farther away from the crowd and my beloved family, I felt a searing pain. When I could not see them anymore, I looked up at the sky. The stars were fading, and it was very still, except for the clip-clop of the horses' hooves.

Passing the familiar houses on well known streets was eerie and unreal. There was a feeling of finality about this parting. A fervent prayer welled up in my heart, "Please Hashem, don't let anything happen to them!"

Chapter Nineteen

BOARDING THE TRAIN TO BUDAPEST SHOULD HAVE BEEN EXCIT-
ing, but we were in a trance. When the train stopped at one
of the stations, it was already daylight, and there on the
platform were Aunt Gitel and her eldest son Yitzchak to say
good-bye. Mamuka was tearful but composed. In Budapest
we settled in at a friend's home, and then we set off for the
American consulate.

Rivkah and I had been in that big city, the capital of
Hungary, once before to take care of our papers for the trip.
Since it was a nice day, we started to walk so we could see as
much as possible. After a while, we were all very tired, so
Mamuka hailed a taxi. The driver took us for a long ride.
Then he stopped exactly where he had picked us up and
pointed to the consulate across the street. Of course, Mamuka
had to pay him, because it was her mistake; if she would have

looked around carefully she would have seen where we were. She called it paying *rebbe gelt.*

At the consulate another cloud burst. Rivkah's eyes, red and inflamed from crying, had to be examined for trachoma. We had to leave that evening by train to Cherbourg, but the doctor who could give the okay would only be in the following day. "It is better to find out now," they told us, "than to be sent back from France."

The announcement that she could not go with us came like a thunderbolt. "If Rivkah can't go with us," said Mamuka, "we will wait together for the verdict, and with the help of Hashem all three of us will go together."

It could not be worked out that way. There were no timetables to pick and choose from. All those who were *shomer Shabbos* were scheduled to go the day before the others to arrive at Cherbourg before *Shabbos.*

The American representative at the consulate was very nice and helpful. Everything was done to make our situation more bearable. Contacts were made, rabbis consulted, and it was decided that we would go and Rivkah stay. We were assured that if after examination the doctor said she was fine, she would be assigned a female passenger as chaperon till Cherbourg.

Sadly, we went back to our friends' home. They tried to reassure Mamuka. "In case, Heaven forbid, Rivkah has to return home," they said, "we will see to it that she arrives there safely."

I stubbornly refused to think of that possibility.

At the train station that evening, the three of us clung together, sobbing unashamedly. With tears in her eyes, the lady from the consulate said to me, "Don't cry. You'll ruin your beautiful eyes also." That made me cry even more, because it was said so kindly.

The trip from Budapest to Cherbourg was unpleasant. The train was packed, and at borders the papers and luggage were checked. The man from the consulate who was traveling with us saved us from opening suitcases—a good thing, since the officials were very rude, and we saw how those cases that were opened for inspection were turned upside down and inside out.

At one point, someone got off the train, so we had three seats for the two of us. I sat on the floor and insisted that Mamuka stretch out and try to sleep a little. She did, and I dozed.

Soon a group of boys and girls carrying skis and talking very loud German came on and told me to wake Mamuka. I tried to tell them in broken German that Mamuka was very tired and not feeling well, but when one of the young men started to shake her by the shoulder, I pushed him aside and helped her sit up. Then I quickly sat down next to her so that only one of them was able to sit.

On the way there was a stop in Paris, where we were put into cars and taken to a hotel that seemed very grand to my unsophisticated eyes. Eating food that was not prepared in our kitchen was strange to me. At the spa restaurant that Mamuka had run (one other way she had once tried to earn money), we were on the other side of the counter. I was full of admiration for Mamuka, who handled it as if she had been born to it.

Friday morning, we arrived in Cherbourg. As soon as we were settled and Mamuka had prepared her candles, we ate what she thought we could eat. Although the hotel was kosher, Mamuka was always extra careful.

Our group of *shomer Shabbos* people was to be taken out in a small boat to see the *Queen Mary* that day. We were to board the *Queen Mary* on *Shabbos*, and in order to do so according to *Halachah*, we had to take that short trip on Friday.

Mamuka was worried about my pink-eye, so in the meantime we set out to find a pharmacy where we could buy eye drops. We had directions, and luckily, it wasn't far. Unfortunately, though, no one there understood what we wanted.

Mamuka tried to make herself understood in Yiddish and Hungarian. That failing, she used pantomime, pointing to my red eye and then to my red collar. The young man behind the counter still did not understand what was needed. Suddenly, a young lady stepped forward and asked in broken Yiddish if she could be of help.

Indeed, Hashem had sent us an angel in the form of a vacationing nurse from New York's Beth Israel Hospital. After looking at my eye she said, "It's nothing to worry about," and told the druggist what to give us. Since the man wouldn't take our currency, she paid for it herself, assuring us that the amount was very small.

When we got back to the hotel, we were taken out in a boat to see the *Queen Mary*. The beauty of the liner was staggering. Our "angel" was also on the trip, so we had someone to share our wonder with. If a nurse from America was *shomer Shabbos*, America couldn't be all that bad.

That evening, when Mamuka lit the candles, I saw she was trying very hard not to cry. I had double portions of fish and plenty of *challah*, but Mamuka did not eat much. By then, Mamuka, who made friends easily, found out from others that they, too, expected beloved ones to arrive on *Shabbos*. She did not talk about Rivkah.

I fell asleep that night with the words "I hope Rivkah comes" on my lips. The next thing I knew, Mamuka was gently shaking my shoulder. Knowing I needed the rest, she had *davened* and waited to wake me as late as possible.

By the time I got to the table I had butterflies in my stomach. "I want to start my diet right now," I said.

That brought a tiny smile to her lips, for she knew I never refused food.

Our guide walked us to the train terminal, and I was agog at the hugeness of it. Together with many other people, we were standing on a high balcony looking down, watching train after train come in and disgorge hundreds of small figures. I wondered how we were going to find Rivkah, even if she did come.

Suddenly, I spotted my hat and coat. Although I could not see the face, I started jumping up and down screaming, "Rifi! Rifi!" The young woman holding her arm noticed me first. Nudging my sister, she pointed up at us. "Look, Erzsebet," she said. "You are up there!"

Our guide took us to a large room where we met, hugged, laughed, cried and hugged again.

"Being left alone in Budapest was a horror," Rivkah told us. "Then I felt that having to board the train on *Shabbos* was the ultimate punishment for all my sins. But it got worse. When I tried to *daven*, the gentile chaperon told me not to do so openly. And each time there was an inspection of luggage or papers, I was filled with fear that I would never see you again."

From then on, everything seemed to happen in a wink. We walked back to the hotel, gathered our things, walked back to the pier and got on the small boat that was to take us to the *Queen Mary*. I was so busy talking that I did not notice we arrived. All we could see was a gray wall a mile high with a gaping entrance. Before I could collect my thoughts, we were ushered onto the ship, where officers in gorgeous uniforms greeted us. Just behind the officers was a familiar figure. Hands behind his back, in his long beard and *Shabbos* clothes, stood Mr. Grossman from our town. Actually, we already knew he was in England, but this was some surprise. It was good to see him.

We were shown into a beautiful little cabin with all kinds of comforts. I couldn't wait to see everything. No sooner did we put our things down than I wanted to go exploring. Afraid that I would get lost, Mamuka came along.

Hashem works in mysterious ways. Parting with our family had been very, very painful, and leaving Rivkah behind had been devastating. The miracle of seeing her on that crowded platform and the joy of having her with us again eased our pain and made parting with Chayah Sarah, Raidl and Eisik a little easier to bear. As I quietly thanked Hashem, Mamuka said, "Dear children, don't ever forget how wonderfully good Hashem is."

Holding hands, we roamed the ship from deck to dining hall and gazed at the windows of the boutiques. We even wandered into first class, where we were politely but firmly asked to go back to our humble quarters.

We stood at the railing as the *Queen Mary* left port. That was the last time any of us was able to stand for the next two days. First, Rivkah took to her bed with dizziness and nausea. Mamuka and I went to the dining room and halfheartedly pushed some food around our plates. It was painful to look at all that beautiful food and not be able to eat. The little we did eat did not take long to come back up. Rivkah was sent a tray, but just looking at the food made her sick. I was the only one who wasn't too sick, but I stayed in to be with the others. Mamuka always enjoyed my singing, and now it eased the boredom of staying in all day.

On the third morning, they were well enough to get dressed and venture upstairs. When the waiter saw how green Rivkah was, he tried to tempt her with all kinds of goodies. He peeled a huge banana and clowned around with it, begging her to take one bite. When she refused, he pushed the banana into his own mouth. The only bananas I had ever seen before were the ones Mamuka brought home from Budapest. They were slightly brown, and by the time we threw them out they had an odor that, at that moment, came back to me and caused me to gag.

By the time we reached New York, Rivkah had lost many pounds. But that didn't happen to me. Fat somehow seemed to stick to me.

When we were finally up and around, we spent a lot of time on deck playing games or just sitting in deck chairs, despite the cool weather. We saw movies and watched the nightly dances. By the time we returned to our cabin, Mamuka and Rivkah were tired enough to retire. I was always ready for more.

For us small town kids, the trip was a continuous wonder. Before we came on board I had never seen a black person, only in advertisements, and I thought black people were the product of someone's lively imagination.

We experienced a fierce, frightening storm. From the porthole in our cabin, it looked like the world was coming to an end.

Our nights were disturbed by screams of horror. The first time we heard them, we all ran out to see what had happened. No one was outside. Thinking that help might be needed, Mamuka gently knocked on the door of the cabin next to ours. The woman who opened the door told us, "My fifteen-year-old son was held and tortured by the Germans. He's had nightmares ever since."

Five days and nights of constant tension and excitement culminated in the unbearable anticipation of arrival. On Wednesday morning, we got up very early to pack in order to be the first passangers at the ship's railing to see the Statue of Liberty.

We stared at Miss Liberty's majesty in awe. We were finally in America.

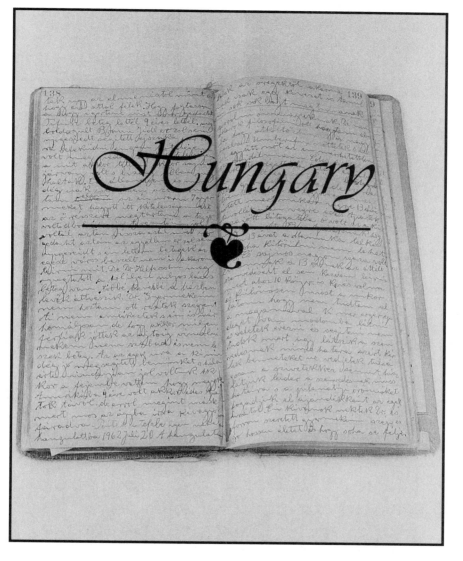

Hungary

Mamuka (Lena Brown) as a *kallah*.

The Weinstock family shortly after Tatika left for America.
left to right: Feige, Channah, Chayah Sarah, Raidl, Rivkah,
Gitel, Mamuka and Eisik
This was the first of many family pictures sent to America.

Tatika before he left for America.

Uncle Avraham Meyer Brown who became a father figure to the Weinstock children.

Mamuka and Eisik

Chayah Sarah, Mamuka, Rivkah and Gitel

Mamuka and the children outside the storefront extension
of their new house in Szemihaly

The Weinstock family: (*left to right*) Feige, Eisik, Gitel,
Chayah Sarah, Mamuka, Rivkah, Raidl and Channah

Rivkah and Gitel

left: Channah and
Chayah Sarah

bottom: (*left to right*)
Eisik, Suri, Feige,
Mamuka, Channah,
Raidl, Rivkah and
Gitel

Chayah Sarah at the well in
the yard

above (*left to right*):
Gitel, Feige, Rivkah
below (*center*): Raidl

Rivkeleh Klien, Chayah
Sarah and cousin

Channah in front of house

Rivkeleh Klein

Chayah Sarah

Eisik before his marriage

Raidl

Chayah Sarah as a *kallah*

Gitel and
Rivkah at
Chayah
Sarah's
wedding

Chayah Sarah and Shaya

Shaya

bottom right: Shaya after his first haircut

Eisik and friend on furlough from Hungarian army

The Klein cousins. Eisik's future *kallah* is in the back row.

1937

Above: Gitel and her classmates (Gitel is in the top row, fourth from right)

Left: Feige, Channah, Rivkah and Gitel (1937)

America

Chapter One

IMPATIENTLY WE WENT THROUGH THE FORMALITIES OF DISEM-
barking and into the waiting arms of our family. Everyone
talked at once amidst hugs, tears and laughter as we piled into
a taxi.

The sight of Tatika's tiny apartment in Washington
Heights made us laugh. The entire place could have fit into
one room of our home in Szemihaly. Although my father
knew we would need a larger place to live in, he wanted
Mamuka to make the choice. We hardly unpacked; there was
no room to put anything. Besides, we hoped to move in a few
days.

Feige and Channah could hardly wait to take us out and
show us around. Besides, we wanted our parents to have a
chance to talk alone. Having been in the United States six
months, they were old Americans. It was a misty evening with

a slight drizzle, and the wet pavement reflected the neon lights. The stores were still open, and I was awed by my sisters' ability to negotiate for bread, milk and eggs.

Tatika had been living in Washington Heights to be near his business on 116th Street. But Mamuka said she would like to live someplace where she could manage in Hungarian and Yiddish until she learned English. So Tatika contacted his friend Mr. Ehrenreich, who lived in Williamsburg, and we set out for his neighborhood. Armed with a lemon to smell or suck in case of nausea, we took our first, unforgettable trip through the New York subway system.

Mr. Ehrenreich took us up and down Lee Avenue and proudly pointed out the few stores that were *shomer Shabbos*. With all the "Apartment to Let" signs on houses, we had no trouble finding a four-room apartment on Rodney Street for twenty-five dollars a month. Within ten days of our arrival in New York, we moved to Williamsburg.

It was a week before *Pesach*. Painting was out of the question. There was only time to clean up as best we could and put curtains on the windows. Mamuka tried to work magic practically from nothing. She pulled embroidered tablecloths and doilies out of suitcases, but her efforts were not very successful.

The bathroom had hot running water. Despite clanking pipes and an occasional roach, the tub was large and comfortable. After the wooden tub in Hungary, and the necessity of hauling and heating water for the bath, this was luxury.

Mamuka asked Tatika if he would prefer for her to wear a *shaitel*, as she had done before he left. He replied, "To me you look beautiful as you are." Mamuka chose to stay in the *tichel*.

My parents were among the very first members of the new Tzelemer *kehillah*. They made friends our first *Shabbos* in the

Tzelemer *shul*. Another lady who came to *shul* the first time that *Shabbos* took one look at Mamuka and started to cry. "In Munkacs," she said, "I wore a black *tichel* on my head like you do. But when I reached Paris, my children said, 'You can't go to America like that,' and they bought me a blond *shaitel* and pink hat. Now, if *you* can wear a black *tichel* in America, so can I!"

Mamuka's assurance to Uncle that she would make America over had begun to come true.

In the beginning, Tatika did not let us go to Manhattan alone. Since we wanted to see the great world, one Sunday he took us to the city where, like tourists, we took photographs in front of the tall buildings to send back to our family in Hungary.

Chapter Two

WE DIDN'T LIVE ON RODNEY STREET FOR LONG. IT WAS DILAPI-
dated, and rather than renovate it, we took another apartment that Mamuka noticed being remodeled on Lee Avenue.
The rent for this high first-floor apartment above Lam's
Butcher Shop was forty-five dollars a month, a week's earnings for Tatika. Since money was sent back to Hungary for the
family and the needy, we would have to watch our spending
very carefully in order to afford it. The apartment had four
rooms, a nice new bathroom and no roaches. There was a
step-out roof from the small kitchen where a *sukkah* could be
built. We waited impatiently for the day we could move in.

That summer, Rivkah and I were enrolled in special
classes for new immigrants in the local public school, and
Mamuka went looking for jobs for Feige and Channah. When
she proudly told employers that her daughters would not

work on *Shabbos*, the answer was always a flat "No." One employer advised Mamuka to let the girls go job hunting on their own. "This is America," he proclaimed.

Mamuka had an idea. "Don't say anything about *Shabbos* unless you are asked," she told Feige and Channah. "By Friday, they will see how good you are and you won't be fired." Mamuka's confidence in her children almost worked, except that my sisters had never used an electric sewing machine. When they put their foot on the pedal to pump, it ran away from them.

A solution was found. A factory machine was rented with the option of paying it up monthly if we eventually wanted to buy it. It was fun taking turns at it and mastering the monster.

Feige and Channah soon found employment as machine operators in a bathing suit factory, for which they were paid five dollars a week. To go through that first week until Friday afternoon not knowing whether the job would still be there the next week was nerve-racking. At night, they went to school to learn English.

Mamuka wanted to go out to work, too, but Tatika wouldn't hear of it. Instead, an arrangement was made to bring work home for her. Feige and Channah brought home heavy bundles of cut bathing suit sections and took them back finished. Nothing came easy, but no one complained. We had worked hard in Europe, too.

The family's earnings were pooled. Tatika paid all the bills, and we received pocket money.

Housekeeping was a shared effort. Rivkah and I helped with the shopping and cleaning after school. To go shopping, either we used our limited Yiddish or someone stepped forward to translate our Hungarian into English or Yiddish.

All of us watched pennies. We carried bags of groceries home ourselves to save the five-cent tip. Instead of paying five cents to take the trolley on the corner to the East Side, we walked to the bridge and crossed for three cents, two pennies saved!

Being that the merchandise in America was usually priced ninety-nine cents, sixty-nine cents, etc., I quickly accumulated fifteen pennies from shopping trips. My conscience would not let me keep the money. I offered it to Mamuka, and she told me to buy something for myself. I bought one pound of Bing cherries, red and luscious. Although there were cherries in the house, along with plenty of other food, to have a whole pound of them to myself was a luxury.

Mamuka bought a spring coat. When she saw the same coat on someone else, and heard that the other lady had paid exactly half the price, Mamuka went back to the store with the two coats and the bill of sale. She got her money back.

Although travelling to Manhattan was not easy in the beginning, Mamuka was never daunted. Rather than take the wrong turn, she asked for information in Yiddish, and if the person she asked did not understand, he looked around for someone who did. After our experiences with the Hungarian *zsandarn*, it took time for us to accept Tatika's statement that "the best person to ask is a policeman."

Mamuka urged everyone to shop in *shomer Shabbos* stores, even if the items cost somewhat more, in order to support *shomer Shabbos* people.

By nature, I was a happy person, always singing and, when possible, dancing. Mamuka once wrote to Raidl asking, "Will Giteleh ever grow up? She never talks but sings, and she never walks but dances." Raidl wrote back, "Please don't rush her. Life will make her grow up soon enough." It upset me that many times when I came home in the afternoon, I found Mamuka tearful, thinking of the children she had left behind. By the time the others came home, she had pulled herself

136

together and put on a good front. That is why I began to insist on going out to work.

We always knew that not all Jews were religious. As children, we talked in whispers about the dentist and the doctor who were not *shomer Shabbos*. There was a farmer who came to say *Yizkor* on *Yom Kippur*; he parked his cart some distance from the *shul* and walked the rest of the way. But when we saw the multitude in America who separated being Jewish from *Yiddishkeit*, we began to understand why Uncle Avraham Meyer had been so worried about our coming out of the *shtetl*.

One woman told us that when she came to America in the early 20's, she was a sixteen-year old staying with non-religious relatives. The first time they took her by subway across the Brooklyn Bridge on *Shabbos*, she was afraid the bridge would collapse. The next time was easier.

An acquaintance who was not too observant was constantly boasting about her grandfather who was a rabbi. "It's very nice to be proud of our grandparents," Mamuka told her. "But do they also have reason to be proud of us?"

Afterwards, Mamuka was upset because she might have hurt the woman's feelings. "Never utter hasty words," she admonished us. "Once said, they cannot be retracted."

If Mamuka had not been with us, we might well have strayed and taken the "easy way out" like so many others who left the *shtetl*. Sometimes trying to stay on the right *derech* required doing major battle against a powerful force. We were labeled old-fashioned and backward. When my parents were looking for a *shidduch* for Feige, people were amazed that a young girl was planning to wear a *shaitel*. Mamuka was advised to remove her own *tichel* and black stockings. For the sake of *tznius*, she would buy three of the same garment, and use one to make sleeves that covered the elbows and to fix

137

open necklines. When we showed up in identical dresses, we were teased about getting them at fire sales.

Making friends was a slow and painful process. Mamuka's view on acquiring friends was simple: "Try to associate with people from whom you can learn. Life is too short to waste doing the wrong things." Eventually, we had a lovely group of European girlfriends. With American acquaintances, though, we had some problems. They called me "Mokky" or "the *greene*." Whenever I said, "I don't speak English," I was asked, "What does 'I don't know' mean?" I would answer *"Ich veis nisht."* They would laughingly reply, "You see? You know English already, Mokky."

Although it was said in fun, it hurt nevertheless. I felt that we were not accepted in this beautiful world that we had adopted so eagerly. As we tried even harder to learn the language of our new country, our Yiddish also improved.

Chapter Three

THAT FALL, BEFORE WE MOVED TO OUR NEW APARTMENT, THERE was a cold spell. At five o'clock one morning, we woke up to a racket of banging and hissing. I pulled myself out of bed and ran into the living room, where I collided with Channah. Tatika was laughing, and Mamuka was boiling water for coffee. At first we chatted, enjoying our togetherness and the miracle of heat coming from the iron radiators. Eventually, we fell silent, each absorbed in his own thoughts.

That morning Mamuka had an appointment with someone at HIAS who would take her to see a senator about getting Eisik out of Hungary. She was promised that inquiries would be made. Months later, the answer came back that no male over the age of eighteen would be permitted to leave the country. We were not surprised, only very sad. Even though Mamuka knew the answer in advance, she still had to try.

MAMUKA

Our new apartment on Lee Avenue was an improvement over the old one. Channah, Rivkah and I shared one large bed that took up almost the entire bedroom, and Feige, being the oldest, slept on the living room couch. There wasn't much privacy, but we adjusted.

The machine Mamuka rented had its niche in the living room, and it came in very handy. Countless young girls came to our apartment to learn to run it and practice on it.

Although Mamuka wanted me to stay in school, I convinced her that it would be better if I worked. There was not much else for girls who came to America at that time besides the factory. When I finally received my working papers, I joined Feige, Channah and many of our friends in the bathing suit factory as a floor worker. To work in those sweat shops, one needed a lot of faith in better things to come.

One day, I came home crying, and told Mamuka I had been fired because I would not work on *Shabbos*. "Please don't do anything about it," I begged her. "Just let it go, and I'll look for another job.

Luckily, we had no phone in the house yet, so she was not able to call the shop to give them a piece of her mind.

Soon after, Feige got a job learning how to make dresses in a Long Island dress factory, and in the same place, Rivkah was shown how to use a special machine for button holes. This was a union shop where the pay was fifteen dollars for a thirty-five hour week. It was worth the two hours traveling time on the subway.

Meanwhile I had been staying home because my parents refused to let me work for five dollars a week. During that time I convinced Mamuka to buy me a piece of material and a pattern, and my sewing career began. That first dress was a disaster, but Mamuka said, "If you decide to wear it, then do so with pride. After all, you made it!"

When I finally joined my sisters in the Long Island factory as a floor worker, I was just biding time until I could sit at a sewing machine.

Eventually, we got a telephone, which ranked with the refrigerator and central heating as a great American miracle.

Early in 1941, the boss's wife called us into her office to take a phone call. Worried and frightened, the three of us tumbled into the tiny room. Feige took the phone, listened to Mamuka's voice, and said, "*Mazel tov.*"

It was the saddest good news I ever heard. Eisik was married! Mamuka had received a telegram with a terse announcement and a promise that "letter will follow." I stumbled back to the niche where I worked. The dresses hanging all around me allowed me to cry in privacy. I didn't know for whom to feel more sorry—Mamuka, who missed the wedding of her only son, or Eisik, whose *barmitzvah* wish was never granted. He had neither father nor mother at his wedding.

We worried about Mamuka being alone that day, but we need not have. Tatika went home as soon as he heard the news. When we got home, we drank *l'chaim* and all of us cried.

The letter which finally came explained that Eisik did not see the purpose of waiting any longer for his release from Hungary. So he had married Rifkeleh and then taken the most painless way to let us know—after the fact. He described the wedding in detail and assured us he was very happy.

In a letter which followed Eisik's wedding, Raidl wrote, "You would not believe it! Eisek, who was never expected to do anything, is actually helping his wife Rifkeleh clean the house."

That letter was one of the last we received from our family. We sent telegram after telegram, reply paid. Since I supposedly knew how to write English, I would go with

Mamuka to the telegraph office, fill out the forms and hand them to the man behind the counter. The first time, he read the form and said with a smile, "You want to receive a message, not a massage."

Europe was in chaos, and no one knew what was going on in Hungary. When no message came back from the family there, we knew things were not good. But we had no idea how bad things were.

America's declaration of war in December of 1941 came as a shock. Now postal connections between Hungary and America were officially severed.

The war brought more job opportunities and better pay, and we all earned much more.

A friend of Channah got her a job in a blouse factory, and I finally got my wish and went to work at a sewing machine in the same shop.

For days and weeks, I was doing section work, endlessly sewing on pockets until I graduated to setting in sleeves, collars and zippers. Each time I started something new, Mamuka's words accompanied me, "If you try hard enough you can do anything."

I felt proud when I finally began to sew dresses and eventually became a sample maker. Soon, I was designing and making my own clothes as well.

With everyone earning more money, Mamuka was able to stop sewing for factories. Instead, she devoted herself to charitable work. Her pet project was the Tzelemer Yeshivah.

The *yeshivah's* location on South First Street made it hard for little children to get there. No one had cars, and it was a very long walk. Mamuka hit on the idea of a school bus. It took some doing, but the happy day came when the bus, loaded with children accompanied by *rabbeim*, stopped in front of our house. They insisted that Mamuka put on a coat and accompany the children on this first trip. It was a bitterly cold day and snow covered the ground, but the children rode to *cheder* in comfort. The initiation of the first *chassidic* school bus was recorded by camera.

In the early Forties, the Tzelemer *kehillah* arranged a surprise party to honor Mamuka for her ceaseless work on its behalf. There was a huge turnout. Mamuka looked as if she wanted to hand the honor over to someone else, but it was evident that she was deeply moved.

Mamuka never expected anything in return for her charitable endeavors; it was enough for her to see people happy. She fled from honor and always sat at the foot of the table, but honor pursued her. Once I overheard someone remark, "Wherever Mrs. Weinstock sits is the seat of honor."

Chapter Four

MAMUKA EXPLORED EVERY POSSIBILITY OF GETTING MONEY TO the family in Hungary. One way was through a company that would deliver funds to the family from people who wanted to get theirs out of Hungary, and we would deposit funds for those people in the U.S. But the time came when the company notified us that they were not able to deliver; the addressee was unknown.

We were in limbo, not knowing what was happening. The uncertainty and waiting were nerve-racking. It was torture to watch Mamuka look for the mailman even though we did not get any mail for years. Most of the time she tried to hide her anxiety and not discuss it, but it was a situation that was impossible not to think or talk about.

We had some happy moments, too. Feige got married—yes, she put on a *shaitel*—and then Channah.

My parents bought a house on Williamsburg's Penn Street. We used two floors for ourselves; the third floor was rented. In the attic, Tatika took one small room for his shop; the rest of the apartment was given to a needy couple.

Some of the furniture came with the purchase of the house, including the beds. The first night after moving in, Rivkah and I slipped between the clean sheets and, being very tired, we promptly fell asleep—only to wake up to a horrible itching. I scratched my arms and legs, and all of a sudden, two hands were not enough. The noise I was making woke Rivkah, and she snapped on the light. We stared at each other bleary-eyed and noticed that each of us was covered with red blotches. Then Tatika came in to investigate. "Bed bugs!" he exclaimed. He ran downstairs and returned with a spray can. After Tatika had sprayed the mattresses thoroughly, we were able to sleep the rest of the night, despite the strong smell of the spray.

Gabriel Heather's nine o'clock radio news program became a nightly ritual. In March of 1944, we heard him say in a sad voice, "Tonight is a dark night for Hungarian Jews." Unable to comprehend the full meaning, we feared that the people were cold and hungry. We had too much blind faith in our President Roosevelt to think that the destruction of European Jewry would be allowed to take place.

One *Shabbos* in 1945, when we least expected it, we received a very thin air mail letter from Europe. The address, in pencil, read: "Sam Weinstock, Brooklyn, America"—just that and nothing else. It could only have arrived by Divine guidance. The sender was Agi Kohn, someplace in Germany. All day *Shabbos* the letter lay on the table, and every once in a while, one of us went and stared at it.

Agi was a young girl from our home town, the sheltered youngest daughter of an esteemed, influential family. What was she doing in Germany? Why was she writing to us? And if her letter came, why didn't we receive mail from our family? The questions were endless.

The letter was not opened until my father came home from *shul* and made *Havdalah*. Mamuka took it with shaking hands but then gave it to Tatika to open for fear she might tear it.

There was one thin, tear-stained page with barely legible lines:

I was able to get hold of a stub of pencil. We were taken from our homes. My mother couldn't bear it. She went out of her mind and was taken away. My brother David Leib is alive. We are trying to find the rest of the family. About yours we know nothing. Please help in any way you can.

After the initial shock wore off, a telegram was sent to Agi in the Displaced Persons' Camp to let her know that help was on the way.

After that letter, we knew that something terrible had happened, but we did not know exactly what. We were afraid to talk about it; we were even afraid to look at each other. I often thought of intercepting the next letter so that Mamuka would not see it. But I realized it would only prolong the torture of uncertainty. To think was destructive; it was a relief to do something. We got busy.

We would have liked to send Agi a large package full of everything, but we were limited to a regulation-size overseas box. We packed cocoa, tea, chocolate, stockings, tuna, sardines, air mail stationary, pens and a small *siddur*, and prayed that the box would get to her. It did. We also sent a letter asking for more details. Even then we knew very little of what went on in Europe. There were only rumors.

Using information she had gleaned in her attempts to get her children out of Europe, Mamuka began to work on sending off affidavits in which the Weinstocks vouched for the support of the new immigrants so they would not be a burden to the country. When she needed the help of an organization, Michael Tress graciously came to her aid.

After a few months, a second letter came from Agi. The package was like manna from heaven. What I couldn't use I sold. There are other girls without families at the same camp. Please send them packages.

She included a list of names. With her new pen, Agi wrote about deportations, concentration camps and gas chambers. She still had not heard about our family.

Even after reading Agi's letter, we did not want to believe that our family was no more. Mamuka cried a lot, worrying that her children might be cold or hungry. Whenever Mamuka saw a lavish smorgasbord at a wedding, she would say, "A family could live for a week from what is thrown away in leftovers." But never could she believe what had really happened.

The reality was like a bucket of cold water thrown in our faces every time we thought of it. It came in waves, ready to drown us in its wake. The shock was devastating.

Mamuka suffered a mild heart attack and was in bed most of the summer. Since visitors were restricted, the family stayed with her as much as possible. Rivkah gave up working to take care of her full time. I sang her songs that Eisik used to sing. When I saw tears, I was alarmed. "I'm fine," said Mamuka. "I enjoy listening."

The doctor said it was all right to cry, so I went on singing.

MAMUKA

Just after Mamuka got over her heart attack, Rivkah became engaged, and we got busy with preparations.

One evening in August, Mamuka was in bed resting, and we were all relaxing with her, making small talk. Suddenly, we heard bells and sirens. People spilled out into the street, hugged each other and shouted, "The war is over!" Boys were running to and fro selling newspapers with big headlines: "War Over." Inside there was no story—there hadn't been time to write it. Tatika switched on the radio, and on every station we heard the same unbelievable announcement: "The war is over."

Chapter Five

AFTER THE INITIAL CAUTIOUS ELATION AND TEARS OF HOPE, WE sat in silence. It was broken by Mamuka. "There is no sense sending a telegram. Where would we send it to? Agi is in Germany. Where could the children be?".

Hopes of hearing from them started to burn in our hearts.

Package sending to Agi's girlfriends in the D.P. camp snowballed into an industry. The money came from Tatika's pocket and Mamuka's collection. Tatika did the shopping with the help of one of us sisters. We packed and addressed at night, sometimes into the early hours of the morning.

At the peak of these activities, we were packing and mailing sixty odd packages weekly. Using a pushcart borrowed from the grocer, Tatika would push and I would steady the pile. We did not have to stand in line. The staff at the post office knew us and always welcomed us with cheers.

At times, the mailman brought our mail in a special little sack because there were so many thank-you's for the packages, replies to our letters and requests for packages or just mail.

As soon as the doctor let, Mamuka started writing endless letters to *kehillos* all over Hungary where she had friends and relatives in the hope that the *kehillos* had reopened and would be able to provide her with the addresses of these people.

Some of these letters were answered, but the joy at finding a person alive was clouded by the survivor's inevitable accounts of the missing and dead. From Szemihaly came a letter from the only person who had returned. He asked for money to put the cemetery in order. It had been desecrated, like everything else Jewish.

The survivors were emotionally starved. One young woman wrote, "I know it is a myth that in America money grows on trees. I don't need or expect anything. Just write to me sometimes, if you can."

Occasionally, there were rewards. In a routine letter to a cousin, Mamuka mentioned that we had just received mail from his mother, Aunt Gitel. The answer that came was a surprise. "If I were only close enough to kiss the hand that wrote to me that my mother is alive!"

Agi and her brother decided to go to Palestine, but others came to America. Whether they came on the affidavits Mamuka sent or otherwise, people knew that anyone who needed a place to stay could come to the Weinstocks. If there were not enough beds, room for another mattress would be found somewhere on the floor.

Shortly after a young couple moved into our attic apartment, I didn't find enough linens to change the beds. When I asked Mamuka about it, she said, "The people upstairs have no money to buy linens, so I gave them some. It's easier for us to replace the missing ones."

Sometime later, the wife gave birth to twins. The couple did not have money to buy a single carriage, much less a twin one, so Mamuka wrote a letter to the Bilt Rite company explaining the situation. Three weeks later, we received a letter enclosing a gift certificate for a twin carriage.

By the end of 1946, the package sending tapered off because the girls left the D.P. camps to go to various countries. In Sweden, many of them were adopted by generous non-Jewish families. At least two girls who came to us from Sweden said that the *siddurim* they found in their package had saved them spiritually. Just holding a *siddur* and looking at it made them remember who they were and from where they had come. Every one of Mamuka's girls married in the true Jewish tradition.

Toby, one of my old classmates, came to poor relatives in the Bronx. After a while, she went to other relatives in Los Angeles who pressed her to come. When she saw that they were not as religious as her parents, she left. After Hitler's hell, alone, with no one to advise her, Toby gave up wealth and comfort in order to live the way she had learned at her father's house.

There was one girl, though, who said, "If Hashem can do this to my family, then I can't believe in anything."

Mamuka retorted, "The only thing Hitler has no power to strip you of is your *Yiddishkeit*, and you choose to throw it away?"

The girl remained observant as long as she was living in our house; but at the first opportunity, she moved out and gave up her religious observance.

Mamuka never wore much jewelry, but after the war she gave all her jewelry to us except for her wide gold wedding band. To me she gave the diamond ring Tatika had bought with his first earnings in America. "Don't ask me for it again after a hundred twenty," she admonished smilingly. As a child I had admired that ring, and she had told me that after a hundred twenty it would be mine. Too young to understand what she meant, I had asked, "When will that be?"

Chapter Six

WHEN FEIGE MARRIED, SHE LEFT BEHIND AN OLD, WIDE-BRIMMED, navy blue straw hat with yellow ribbons streaming down the back. I hung it on a hook behind the kitchen door and always put it on when I washed dishes. That and singing made the work less tedious. One evening during Rivkah's engagement, I didn't put the hat on. I didn't feel like singing either. Although our house was never empty, and none of my sisters lived more than a block away, the thought of being the only girl at home depressed me. I was going to miss Rivkah terribly. In fact, I missed her already.

Suddenly, Mamuka was standing behind me with Feige's hat in her hand. Gently placing it on my head, she said, "Sing, Giteleh."

The week after Rivkah's wedding, Mamuka and I were sitting in the kitchen putting the finishing touches on the new couple's bedspreads. Rivkah came into the house, and just as she passed the phone it started to ring. She picked up the receiver, said "Hello," and then listened for a long time. Suddenly she turned white and dropped the receiver. I pushed a chair under her, and Mamuka ran for water. When I picked the receiver up from the floor, a strange voice asked, "What happened?"

"My sister fainted," I replied. "What did you tell her?"

By the time she answered, I was painfully aware of Mamuka standing next to me. "How could you give such news over the phone?" I demanded. "Where are you? Where can we come to see you?"

"I'll come to you," she said. "I have your address."

When I hung up, there was a very bitter taste in my mouth, and dryness that made speaking almost impossible. Mamuka looked questioningly at me. "Bad news about the family," I said, choking on the words.

I would have given my life to spare Mamuka the news. But of course there was nothing else to so, so I told her. "Raidl is gone."

The woman arrived shortly by taxi. It turned out she was from our home town. She broke down as she kissed Mamuka. She had tried to explain on the phone who she was, but things had gotten out of hand. She was full of apologies, and we were all crying before she had finished explaining that she was not being crude or unfeeling. She herself had lost her entire family, and so had most other survivors. To find another family member alive was considered a miracle. Everyone wanted to know who had died, how, when and where, and was relieved to be told that someone had actually seen his loved one die. This lady had not imagined that at that time we were still expecting to find our family alive, if not well.

Raidl, she told us, had had an advantageous position

154

working in a camp food warehouse. She had looked well. She was very clever, and people would consult her. When asked, "Raidl, do you think we will ever get out of this?" she would answer, "Yes! But only Hashem knows who and when."

Eight days before the liberation, Raidl was caught smuggling food to some of the other inmates. A few weeks before she would have been shot for the offense. As there was no order anymore, she was thrown into a cell, and in less than a week she was hurled onto the piles of dead and nearly dead.

Since then, whenever I see pictures of the holocaust, I scan those piles of bodies for my sister's face.

We sat *shivah* for half an hour. It seemed so unreal without a *levayah*. We couldn't believe it was actually happening. Afterwards, our search continued.

We looked through endless lists in the hope of finding Chayah Sarah's or Eisik's name. Never fully believing that they could have disappeared without a trace, we kept looking for people who might have run across them. Eventually, we came to learn that it is indeed a relief to know the horrible truth.

Mamuka did not give up trying to find family and friends. She refused to tear her garment and sit *shivah* for Chayah Sarah or Eisik, and no one forced her to. She kept on searching.

We heard about my friend Jolan. An only girl among four boys, she had been cosseted and spoiled. She grew up on silken pillows and was treated as if she were worth her weight in gold. Her baby was three days old when she was dragged from her silken bed, never to see her child again.

Someone told us that Chayah Sarah was seen on "the left," holding her little Shmuly on her arm, while her mother-in-law held the hand of his big brother Shayele. Someone else said that Chayah Sarah's brother-in-law was working at the

155

crematoria. When he saw the family, the grandmother's hand still touching the boy as if trying to protect him, he couldn't bear the anguish and jumped into the fire.

It took some time for us to understand that "the left" meant death. We learned from Mamuka's girls. After work, we did the housework together; we didn't let Mamuka do much of it after her heart attack. Then we would lie down on the mattresses that we all shared. The girls laughed and joked late into the night as they compared notes on the different concentration camps they had been through; and we, eager to find out every detail, asked questions. Crying, I asked how they could laugh about it. "We never want to cry again," they answered, "only to eat, laugh and go on with our lives."

One source had tentative information that Eisik had been taken from home and put into a cattle car headed for a slave labor camp in Russia without being told his destination. When he refused to cooperate, he was shot. Since there was no definite report about Eisik, we continued to hope that by some miracle he would turn up. It was pure torture. Eventually, the rest of us gave up our false hopes, but Mamuka never accepted the loss of her brightest star. We never sat *shivah* for him.

From some surviving cousins who came to America, we learned that Eisik's wife Rifkeleh was expecting her third child when they were taken away; she gave birth in concentration camp. We sadly added Rifkeleh and those three tiny *neshamalach* to our list of the lost.

My cousin Yitzchak went back to Szemihaly to see if anyone had returned. He visited our home and that of my sainted uncle. Our house was a wreck, windows broken, doors pulled off hinges, furniture axed. The wires of the phonograph had been pulled out, and broken records were strewn about together with the remnants of torn *sefarim*.

Uncle Avraham Meyer's estate was also in shambles, with torn *sefarim* strewn all over. As Yitzchak stood there surveying the ruins, he recalled the glory of the house when it was bustling with life. Realizing that his foot was resting on a *sefer*, he slowly bent down and picked it up. With tears running down his cheeks, he opened it, and between the pages he saw strands of Uncle's gray beard. Uncle used to sit and pore over those *sefarim* the better part of every night, nodding when he could not keep his head up anymore.

"There is no compensation for losing children," said Mamuka. "Other bitter memories, like the thirteen years of loneliness or the times I couldn't give another slice of bread to a child, fade when better times come. Life is a struggle we muddle through as best we can. Just when we think we can't go on anymore, a spark of *nachas* comes along and gives us strength to continue."

Many years later, when Channah was killed in a car accident, I felt as if a knife had been plunged into my heart. My only comfort was that Mamuka was not alive to suffer the agony of that loss.

Just as life can hurt, so can it also heal. The sickening feeling that something so barbarous could happen never eases. You never forget, but that sharp, horrible pain does fade a little, ever so slowly. As Mamuka used to say, "The dead are only those who are buried. The rest of us must go on living."

Chapter Seven

MAMUKA PRACTICED WHAT SHE PREACHED AND CONTINUED living in a way that can only be called "brave."

It was important for her to become a citizen. "If you live in a country that you want to make your home," she said, "you must live by its laws."

She practiced hard for the test, but her English was so broken that there was little hope she would pass. At last the big day came for Mamuka and me. Two of her friends came as our witnesses. When we stood in front of the judge, she asked him a question in Yiddish, and he answered her. "You must be here in America a very long time to have such a high position," she said, indicating with her hand the high seat he occupied.

Laughingly he held up one finger and asked, "Who was the first President?"

When Mamuka said it was Washington, he applauded. "And who is the President now?"

He laughed heartily when Mamuka answered, "Roosevelt, till a hundred twenty."

She promised to be a good citizen and gave him her best wishes before being dismissed.

Indeed, she was a good citizen. One day, a small item in the newspaper reported that doctors had diagnosed some cases of smallpox on Long Island. Word quickly spread that vaccinations were available for those who wanted it. In stores and in the street, people could be seen in discussion. Should they go to the trouble of going to a doctor and pay the three dollars (a notable amount in those days) for something uncertain?

Rather than simply taking her own family for shots, Mamuka arranged for Dr. Zeglin and his nurse Sylvia to come to our house one evening to administer the vaccination to the public for a fee of one dollar per person. For hours, men, women and children lined up to receive the shots. For the children, Mamuka provided lollipops; how many of the fees she paid only she knew.

Now that she was no longer working, Mamuka threw herself heart and soul into charity work. She began to sell silver from the house, with profits dedicated to *tzedakah*.

As in Europe, she made fund-raising parties and raffled off embroidered tablecloths or a silver coffee set that someone had donated.

The Tzelemer ladies made a yearly bazaar at which everything sold was solicited. In preparation for that function, our apartment looked like a warehouse. Tatika helped her make order out of chaos by sorting and labeling whenever he could spare an hour. She went to factories and stores and came home so loaded with merchandise that she had to get the owner of the place to either drive her home or deliver the stuff later.

With all her talents, she never learned to speak English well enough. When she came to a place where Yiddish was not understood, she simply said, "Bazaar." She was very successful and seldom came away empty-handed from any place. Whenever possible she took along one of her grandchildren to help carry small parcels.

Often Mamuka could be seen coming out of a store holding a parcel in each hand and pushing another along the sidewalk with her foot. The parcels were never too heavy, for she was mindful of her health. She was sure someone would come along and help her, as someone always did. Wherever she was, drivers would give her a lift to her next destination.

In Williamsburg, Mamuka was something of a landmark, but she was familiar on Fifth Avenue, too. On rainy days, she held out an umbrella, and traffic stopped to let her cross. Sometimes she just lifted her arm, and cars stopped.

If she was not out helping someone, then she was creating handmade door prizes for the next fund-raising affair. She also tried to do *taharahs*. One day, when she came home pale and tired from doing one, she said, "It's nicer to work with the living, even if they are poor."

Although she could not continue to do *taharah*, she spent a lot of time making *tachrichim* with the Tzelemer Rebbetzin and some other ladies. Hers and Tatika's were side by side on a closet shelf in Beechnut baby food boxes.

Once I told her that if and when I would find time, I would like to visit the sick. "I'm happy to hear that you have such high aims," said Mamuka. "*Bikkur cholim* is a big *mitzvah*, but it's not easy. And I might add that if you want to do a good deed, don't wait for 'if and when.' Find the time and do it now."

I remembered Mamuka's warning that visiting the sick is not easy years later, when my husband volunteered as a chaplain and made Beth Israel Medical Center practically his second home. Sometimes, he took me out for a birthday or anniversary only to end up at the hospital. He was able to go from one to another, bringing good cheer in a few minutes, and then going on to the next. When I tried it, I felt I had to stay with each one for hours and wound up crying myself instead of cheering up the sick person.

Mamuka had a way of detecting need. A family with five children was without a father; the mother was a diabetic with one leg amputated. The rooms were spotlessly clean, though shabby. On my regular visits there, I noticed cases of soda under the kitchen sink. We had seltzer for *Shabbos*, but on weekdays we drank water. I asked Mamuka about it.

"Sometimes," she explained, "what looks like a luxury really is not. With a mother sick and no father, the children must have something to make up for the lack, at least in a small way."

I also wondered abut the necessity of gold necklaces and bracelets for poor *kallahs*. In Hungary, collected money was used to buy only the barest necessities, such as two beds and a table with four kitchen chairs, and people in town were advised what household items—linen, pots and pans—to give as wedding gifts. "Like everything else in the world," said Mamuka, "*chessed* also changes. When people's expectations become higher, a poor *kallah* has to be fitted accordingly."

Mamuka knew what was needed where. To some homes we were sent with parcels of linen, to others with food. There were places she would not send money because she knew it would be misspent.

"Never feel righteous about helping those in need," Mamuka would say. "But for the grace of Hashem, we could have been on the receiving end. Giving *tzedakah* is a *mitzvah* that you do for yourself, to build up your credit in heaven. If someone has to put his hand out, make it easier for him by giving graciously."

She never turned anyone away. It pained her not to be able to give people as much as they needed, so she took from the rich to give to the poor. How did she know whether the recipient was truly needy? Mamuka had a simple answer, "Let's say that ten ask, and only one is in need. If you don't give them all, the one who really needs may not get."

Mamuka had a charismatic personality. People knew her and liked her. Even in her simplicity, there was an elegance about her. She was a very outgoing person, always ready to hear a joke or tell one.

Where she got her addresses was a secret known only to her. Once Channah went along with Mamuka on one of her trips uptown. She stopped before a very fancy townhouse on Fifth Avenue.

"Who should I say would like to see Mr. Zackendorf?" asked the doorman.

"Lena and Channah Weinstock," replied Mamuka.

The doorman phoned upstairs. "Mrs. Weinstock may come up alone," came the reply.

A half hour later, Mamuka came out of the elevator with a smile that indicated a sizable sum.

Whereas in Hungary, collecting money for the poor was part and parcel of a wedding, in America Mamuka had to do battle for the privilege. She was asked to leave through one door, and she came back in through another. It was hard going, but she won. Very discreetly, she made her way among the guests, and she built up quite a clientele. Her grandchildren loved to sort and count the coins for *tzedakah* that she brought home.

Whenever we were at the same wedding, she proudly introduced me to some of her clients. After the initial pleasantries, I was dismissed. Once I asked her why. "I am going to ask for *tzedakah*," she explained, "and I don't want you to have hard feelings against people who refuse."

She always carried two handbags. One contained her purse. The other, which was very heavy, contained all her family pictures, some letters and the *tzedakah* money.

Collecting money for *tzedakah* is not easy. Ironically, in her toughest years in Europe, when there was not enough money to feed the children properly, no one had ever accused her of using collected money for herself; yet here in the land of plenty, there were those who did. She just shrugged her shoulders over such remarks and said, "I am not afraid to face my Creator when the time comes." But the knowledge that it bothered us upset her. As children she had taught us to sing, *"Gutt in Sein mishpat is gerecht. Hashem is correct in His judgment."* And we sang it often and loud even when we were grown.

The fact was that she never collected from strangers before she contributed herself and then asked the family. She never felt any need for herself; if we gave her a robe or pocketbook as a gift, she would give it away to someone else who "needed it more." She cut down on her own expenses as much as possible, to the point of writing letters to the family on the back of form letters that had come in the mail, and trying to get rides rather than spend money on taxis.

Mamuka was shocked at the waste of disposable plastic utensils being thrown away after only one use. She would try to find a way to reuse them.

Basically, Mamuka was a healthy lady, but occasionally she complained of stomach pains. Dr. Zeglin, our family physician, put her on a diet and gave her some pills now and then, and she continued her good works. As the years went by, Mamuka began to spend her summers in Spring Valley, which she felt was good for her health. She always looked forward to going, for she had a tremendous clientele there. Tatika never liked to go to the country; he preferred the comfort of his own home.

Once, the car in which she was traveling to Spring Valley skidded and rolled down an embankment. At the bottom, it miraculously righted itself. When everyone scrambled out of the car unhurt, the police officer who arrived at the scene said, "An angel must have been riding with you."

"Indeed," said the passengers, looking at Mamuka.

Mamuka kept a ledger on all her charities. On a few pages of that ledger, she described the misery of the young woman left alone for thirteen years, and the terrible ache for the three beloved children who were left behind and were no more. She always felt guilty about leaving them, although there was no choice. "If only I could wake up," she wrote, "and find that it was a bad dream."

Chapter Eight

GITELEH FINALLY GREW UP, NO ONE KNEW WHEN. EVERYONE was too busy with other things to notice. But facts were facts; it was time for a *shidduch*.

Mechel and I were to be married on June 30, 1947. Two years after the war ended, the horrible pain was dulled somewhat by the *simchah*. I even heard Mamuka say once, "In spite of everything, life is worth living."

Mamuka made time to talk to me and give me sound advice. "To establish a good Jewish marriage," she said, "first comes Hashem, then the spouse, and then parents. If there is a good relationship between a couple, honor for parents comes automatically."

Mamuka always baked *challos* for *Shabbos*. "Remember that a woman has three *mitzvos*," she admonished me. "One is to take off a piece of dough and make the *berachah*. If you have time to bake cake and strength to wash floors, you can certainly find time for this great *mitzvah*."

I found out that it was not only her family she instructed about the *mitzvah* of baking *challos*. Recently, I was visiting with a member of the Skverer Rebbe's family, and she told me the following tale.

During the long summers Mamuka spent in Spring Valley, she often visited the Skverer Rebbe's house. Having grown up in a *rebbishe* atmosphere, she was always attracted to that sort of life. On one such visit, there were a number of young and old ladies present, and the talk turned to cooking and baking. One lady's pride was her cocoa *babke* and cheese danish. Another was an expert at nut cake and light sponge cakes. And so on. Not one mentioned the art of baking *challos*. Mamuka took it upon herself to tell them about the *mitzvah* of baking *challos* for *Shabbos* and proceeded to give instructions on how to do it with the least trouble.

On subsequent visits, she kept urging the Skverer women to bake *challos,* and my source tells me that Mamuka succeeded. For long years it was said, "This is Mrs. Weinstock's recipe."

June of that year was a beautiful, cool month. We were happy about that, because the wedding was to take place at the beautifully renovated Gold Manor, and the air conditioner had not been installed yet. The thirtieth arrived, and so did a heat wave. As we went round seven times under the *chupah*, Mamuka held my right hand tightly in her left, and pictures of her lost children in her right. After the *chupah*, my gown had to be removed and quickly ironed because it was soaked.

After the wedding, there was not a day I did not drop in to see my parents, even if only for a few minutes. Friday evenings were special. Mamuka lit eighteen candles. I did not have to ask why she lit so many. I knew that the additional candles were for her children, children-in-law and grandchildren who perished *al kiddush Hashem* in Hitler's death camps.

After candle lighting, whoever could come over came, with any children old enough to walk. So did all those for whom my parents' house was home. When the men came back from *shul*, they would chat a little; then each collected his own family and went home.

Mamuka was never generous with compliments; for instance, she never told us we were beautiful. So it came as a pleasant surprise when I dropped into Feige's house one afternoon and a lady visiting said, "What a lovely *shaitel*, Gitel. It suits you to perfection," to which Mamuka commented, "Don't you think the face has something to do with it?"

When I was about to give birth to my first, Mechel said, "Let's surprise everyone."

I went along, but it was pure bravado. I would have liked to have Mamuka with me, but since it was *Shabbos*, she would not have been able to accompany me anyway.

After having contractions all Friday night, early in the morning I asked Mechel to get the doctor. After examining me, the doctor said, "I'm going to *shul*; I'll be back later. Nothing is going to happen quickly."

After they left, I got up and started to prepare for the *Shabbos seudah*. We were having company. Channah was in the country, and her husband Michael was our guest.

The doctor cut short his *davening* and came back soon, followed by Mechel. When Michael walked in and sized up the situation, he immediately offered to go get Mamuka. It took the three of us to convince him that he should not go. (When his first baby was about to be born he vomited all over, and Mamuka had to go along to see that he would be okay.)

I served lunch. I did not eat, and neither did Michael. But the doctor and Mechel ate well. While I cleared away leftovers, Mechel went to say *"Gut Shabbos"* to my parents and tell them I did not feel like getting dressed. He was elated that they did not suspect anything. When he returned, the doctor said it was time to go. Mechel went out to Broadway and found a taxi with a gentile driver. Gingerly holding two dollars in my hand, I got into the taxi with the doctor. On the way to Beth Moses Hospital, the driver reassured him, "Don't you worry, Pop, I have four kids and nothing ever happened to me yet. You'll come out of it all right."

The hospital corridor was packed with women who had just given birth and were waiting for rooms. "Because of overcrowding here," we were told, "you will be sent to a different hospital. We will make the arrangements."

The doctor looked at me. "Even if it means having the baby in the corridor," I said, "I'm not going to go anywhere else."

The doctor thought fast and told the hospital there was no time to go anywhere. We were given a small operating room on the fifth floor where there were very sick people. The room had never handled a delivery, and there was no proper equipment. I never saw so much hustling and bustling in my life. By then it was imminent. I was ready, the baby was ready, the doctor was ready, and lo and behold, a nurse flew through the door.

"Hold it!" she yelled triumphantly. "A delivery room was just cleared for Mrs. Greenhut."

I stubbornly refused to go, but it did not help. "It's against the rules," the doctor explained patiently, "to deliver in this room except in emergencies."

"And what is *this*?" I wanted to know.

But I had no strength to argue, and I was transferred. The

nurse kept yelling, "Hold it! Hold it!" They had a good laugh when I yelled back, "You hold it!"

It was worth it when I saw the baby's round, pink face. I watched the nurse string pink beads with "Greenhut" on it and put the beads around her little neck.

Mechel, who walked the long way to the hospital, arrived right after I was settled in a private room on the fifth floor. He ran up the steps, and upon entering the room said breathlessly, "*Mazel tov*, I was told downstairs we have a *yingeleh*."

I looked at him and saw he was not joking. "I don't know what they told you downstairs," I said, "but I know it's a girl."

He looked surprised. "Are you sure?" he asked.

Although he did not say so, it must have been a disappointment to drop all the plans he had made for a *bris* and a *pidyon* on those five flights up.

That one week on the sick floor was a lesson. I could not be thankful enough to Hashem that I was in the hospital to have a baby. The next day, I was off the bed and visiting the sick.

For five days, I could not see little Chayah Sarah; they would not bring the baby to a sick floor. Mechel kept asking me if I had seen her. He was afraid that with all those births, the baby might have been switched.

On the fifth day, I was put into a wheelchair and taken down to the nursery to see my baby. I immediately recognized that little face. When my eyes fell on the pink beads, I burst out laughing. How easy it would have been to reassure Mechel if I had remembered to mention the beads I saw being put around her neck!

When Mamuka came to visit, with deep gratitude she told me, "You did a tremendous *mitzvah* by not letting me know when you went to the hospital."

As the youngest, I had my share of helping my sisters and

babysitting for their children. I was jokingly reassured, "When you get married, we will help you." Their promises were fulfilled all through the years.

Occasionally, I complained to Mamuka about my Chayah Sarah, Minki, Debby, Eliyohu, Raidl or Bela.

"Children are children," she said, "and that's the way it should be. Only sick children, Heaven forbid, are not mischievous. You weren't any better."

When there were discussions about how toddlers lose their cuteness as they grow older, Mamuka would say, "Every phase of a child's growth has its beauty."

To adults, too, she would say, "Enjoy every age for itself, because time goes by fast. The best time of your life should be now; you never know what the future will bring."

Many times I wonder how much happiness my mother actually had during her lifetime. She bore eight children, lost four, and despite all her other problems she still said, "Life was worth living." I believe she was able to think this way because she did not let her personal problems rule her life. With each heartache, with each dissappointment in life, she strived more and more to fill the void with *chessed.*

Chapter Nine

FIFTEEN YEARS AFTER CHAYAH SARAH WAS BORN, MAMUKA GOT sick. It was in Spring Valley, while helping her prepare a meal, that I first noticed she was not her usual energetic self. After clearing up, we sat talking in deck chairs on the lawn.

"Mamuka," I finally said, "let me pack you up and take you home."

She wouldn't hear of it. "I still have a lot of people to see. I wasn't able to do everything I had planned. Don't worry, I'm feeling fine."

I went home with a heavy heart, kicking myself for not insisting, and spoke to Tatika and Feige about it. Feige lived in the same house, and she was there to handle anything that came up, although she worked full time. Once when I was visiting Mamuka, Feige was just coming home. "I can hardly wait to hear her footsteps in the hall," said Mamuka. She immediately apologized for possibly hurting my feelings.

"I understand," I said. "I know you love us all."

Feige was able to talk Mamuka into coming home with her. Mamuka fussed that the season was not yet over, and she had much more to take care of, but admitted that she was not feeling well, so it was probably better for her to be home. Since Dr. Zeglin was no longer alive, I took her to Dr. Rosenberg, who ran some tests and examined her. He did not find anything wrong except a sour stomach, for which he prescribed some pills.

That *Shabbos*, Mamuka had had some kind of an attack, and Feige was downright scared.

The Skverer Rebbe recommended a specialist named Dr. Janowitz. We called first thing Monday morning and were given an appointment for that afternoon as a courtesy to the Skverer Rebbe. I brought Mamuka to the office, and she went through an examination the likes of which I had never seen. I was there to translate: "Hold your breath . . . breathe . . . drink . . . stop drinking . . . lie down . . . sit up." She must have understood these simple instructions, but she wanted me near her for moral support. She had been to doctors many times before, but I never saw her so scared. If I thought the initial examination was bad, it got worse.

Tests finished, I helped her get dressed, and we waited in the outer room. Soon we were called into the doctor's office. He was sitting at his desk, feeding his findings into a small recorder in his hand. I understood very little of it and, thank Heaven, Mamuka none of it. While he was talking he pointed to some areas on the X-rays that were lined up on the walls. The words carcinoma and pancreas stood out like lightning. I glanced at Mamuka and was sure she did not understand. She looked very, very tired—no wonder, after the ordeal she had gone through. I wanted to get her home, comfort her and tuck her into bed so she could rest. But the ordeal was not yet over.

When it was apparent that the doctor was finished with us, the receptionist was summoned to show us out. Everything was done with a certain ceremony. I was one step behind Mamuka, with my hand on the doorknob, when I felt the woman's hand on my arm, like a brace of ice, detaining me. I had the presence of mind to tell Mamuka, "Sit down; I'll be out in a few minutes."

I sat in a chair facing the doctor and listened as he told me what I wanted to avoid hearing at all costs. Eyes tearing, nose running, I looked around for an escape, for someplace where I would not have to hear that Mamuka was terminally ill. The doctor was compassionate. He patiently explained that there were many kinds of treatments and pills, all in the experimental stage, with no proof of beneficial results. He very kindly advised me to leave her alone.

"You are lucky," he said, "that your mother will have a relatively short and painless illness. Humor her. Let her eat when and what she pleases. Let her rest, sleep or be active at her leisure. Don't torture her with treatments that won't help. Let her die peacefully."

I broke down. I had felt it coming since I heard him talk into the dictaphone. I couldn't control it, and I didn't want to. As if on cue, the receptionist entered, handed me a box of tissues and very gently but quite firmly steered me into the washroom. With her arm around me, she said, "Honey, wash your face and control yourself. You can't face Mother in this condition. You don't want her to know how sick she is, do you?"

After she left, I realized she was right; Honey did not want Mother to know how sick she was. I started washing up. Mamuka is dying, I thought, and I should consider myself lucky. I'd better convince myself, because I will have to sell that line to the family. Thinking of the family, a new flood of tears started. The best thing was to stop thinking. But how? Suddenly, the word miracle popped into my mind. Miracles can happen. With that thought I was able to step into the waiting room.

"Mrs. Greenhut," said the receptionist, "here is Mrs. Weinstock's bill."

I was grateful for the bill. Exorbitant though it was, settling it gave me a few more minutes to compose myself. I couldn't face Mamuka. Again, I thought of miracles. Turning around, I said briskly, "Okay, let's go," and scooped up her sweater, my knitting and our handbags.

The first cab I hailed stopped. Even before I settled into the seat, I started chattering about everything that came to mind. When I stopped for a second to catch my breath, Mamuka quietly asked, "What did the doctor say?"

"What? Oh. It's the same old story with your stomach," I said, knowing I was talking too fast and realizing too late that I should have told her this as soon as I came out of the doctor's office. "You will have to take pills and diet."

"He didn't give you a prescription?"

"Oh, shucks, I forgot it. I'll have to call the office and have them send it to us."

For a while, she was silent. I racked my brains for what to say next, but finally decided to say nothing. There was not much traffic, but the trip seemed endless.

"If there's nothing wrong with me, why are you crying?"

I started to sneeze, rub my eyes and cough, aware that I was overdoing the act. "I'm not crying," I said. "Hay fever is awful this season."

I knew she did not believe one word I said.

Please . . . please, no more questions! I silently prayed. I told Mamuka to close her eyes and rest until we got home. She listened to me like a good little child.

Finally, mercifully, we pulled up in front of my parents' house. Tatika was waiting for us at the front door. As he helped us out of the taxi, he asked, "What did the doctor say?"

Mamuka told him what I had told her. I saw that he actually believed her.

How am I going to tell him? Should I tell him? I wondered. I asked Mamuka if she would like to eat something. When she refused, preferring to rest first, I ran up to Feige. Her living in the same house was a blessing. Together we decided that as painful as it would be for him, Tatika should eventually be told.

Leaving Feige in charge, I went to pick up my baby. I took Chayah Sarah for a haircut she wanted for her graduation pictures, but my thoughts were with Mamuka. After Debby pointed out that I had given the wrong reply to a question, I realized I would have to be careful. The necessary things done, I ran the three blocks to my parents' home.

That night, when Mechel came home, I told him the sad news. After a minute of stunned silence, he said, "I would like to talk to the doctor. Maybe you misunderstood because you were upset."

Knowing I was grabbing at straws, we made an appointment and went to see the doctor the next day. He repeated everything he had told me, including that I was lucky.

"You had the gift of your mother for fifteen to eighteen years," he said. "According to her medical history, she had the beginnings of this way back. If she had been diagnosed and treated then, she might not have lived this long."

There was one change. He suggested that Mamuka be checked into Mount Sinai Hospital for additional tests. We knew it would not accomplish anything, but we wanted to do everything possible. We asked her if she would like to go in, and she said yes.

It was a terrible mistake. Mamuka was miserable in the hospital. One of us was there with her constantly during the day; we were not allowed to stay the night. She had a lot of visitors, but her usual interest in people was missing. While the liver biopsy was being done, I heard her moaning from the other side of the door. Holding my hand, the Satmar Rebbetzin shared my misery.

When we were allowed back into the room, we sat and talked. Shortly a man entered and introduced himself as the hospital chaplain. The Satmar Rebbetzin looked from every angle before asking in Yiddish, "Where is your *yarmulka?*"

He took one out of his pocket. "If you are a rabbi," said the *rebbetzin*, "why don't you wear your *yarmulka*? The Pope is not ashamed to wear his!" The *rebbetzin*, who is very short, looked ten feet tall as she defended her religion.

After a heated dialogue, the chaplain bid us a good day and walked out with a red face, wearing the *yarmulka*.

That evening, before I left, Mamuka whispered, "I want to go home."

I spoke to Tatika and the doctor, and the next morning we took her home and gave her the best, gentlest and most loving care possible.

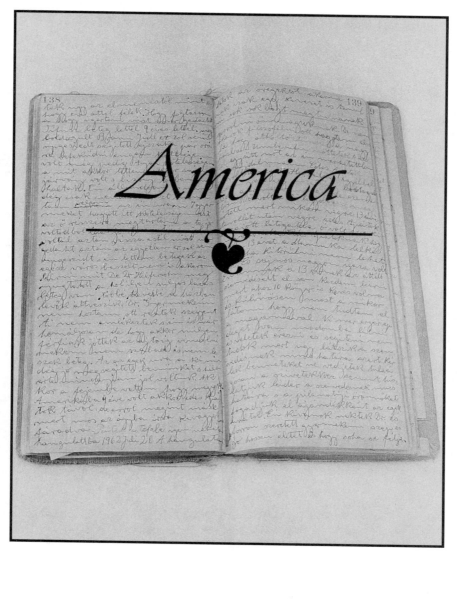

TATIKA

MAMUKA

Gitel, Rivkah, Feige
and Channah

The girls
Williamsburg, 1939

Gitel and Rivkah in front of Manhattan's Rockefeller Center

Gitel before her engagement

Eisik and Rifkeleh

Chayah Sarah and her two children

Gitel and Mamuka

Gitel, Feige, Mamuka, Channah and Rivkah
at cousin's wedding

Mamuka at the
engagement party
of an orphan niece.

Trainer Studios snapped this photograph of Mamuka as she was returning home from collecting at a wedding.

At an engagement party where Mamuka was the *shadchan*

This certificate was presented to Mamuka for her efforts
in acquiring a schoolbus for the Tzelemer Yeshivah.
Mamuka is shown standing beside the bus.

Mamuka's ledger

tök ugy az elmenéstöl mint a
hogy eddig attol féltek. Hogy folytassam
a hogy igértem most Sándor Gyedacht
Tifusz beteg lettél 9 éves lettél meg
boldogult Braun Jidl ez sem
nyugszeedt segitett éjszaka pár órá
ra befeküdni engem kötelessége
volt még pedig Anyai kötelessége
a mit akkor tettem akkor sajnos
járvány volt s bizony többen meg
haltak. Én állandóan és min
dég csak csendesen azt mond
tam velem az én uram 7 gyer
meket hagyott itt kötelességemkt
az ő résszére megtartani s te jó
voltodbol édes jó teremtőm jol
voltál aztán vissza estél miat meg
gedacht aztán az egyetlen ez sem
nyugszeidt s én lettem betegek az
egész város beszélt nem is akarom
leirni mit. De Dr Helfersohn meg
nyugtatott a hol ilyen sulyos lázas
betege van többé kevésbé a házban
levök átveszik. Dr Gyermekeim
nem hoztam ott réztek szégyent
ti nem emlékeztek s én is már
homályosan de hogy akkor milyen
férfiak jöttek az ajtoig vinnölm
nekem nem szabad és nem le
szek beteg. Az az egész ura a Ki mi
dég jó megsegített bennünket a hál

...ar öregekről akarna
...ok egy keveset is tanul
...sok előbújt megtudnának
...mi önmaguknak. De nem
...filozofálni Doll hogytam el
...öttkőltő... ... ... nagy
...Umberzjon ... öttetek s ...
...jött mit az én merhetetlen
...jdalmainen Édes Agotám
...őte vegett. Ha talán legjobbellet
...volt egy ... ... boldogul
...er ... ... de ...
...ő volt a ki legjobban ...
...mert mikor végre 13 ...
...lét után végre édes Agotám
...jött látogatába ő volt az a ki
...mondta Édes Agotámnak hogy
...13 évet a dolunnika lelkén
...ha kitörülni nem lehet
...És sajnos nagyon igaza volt
...mnak a 13 évnek az öttölt
...védésett el sem kezdem leirni
...t ahoz 10 könyv is keves volna
...ilönösen most a mikor
...... hogy nem tudtam el
...magamnidal. Vi mer ezen ap
...et jram modomba látni
...eletek érezni és segiteni nem
...ok mert ugy látszik a szem
...esmnek minda határa azért kér
...benneteket ne vedjetek tulzá
...an a szivetekkber semmit hisz

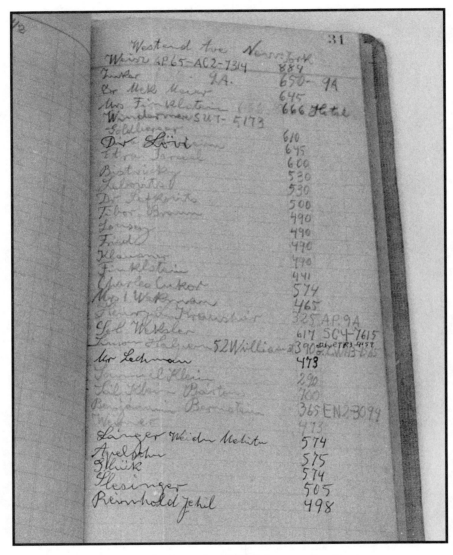

Some of Mamuka's "addresses" where
she raised money for her charities

Chapter Ten

THE BEGINNING WAS THE HARDEST. WE WERE NOT SURE WHETHER Mamuka was aware of how ill she was. Although the many visitors were welcome, we worried that someone might mention the word "cancer."

At first, she made some attempts to go out to raise money. "So much to do," she kept saying. "The need is so great."

But even with someone accompanying her, she could not go far or stay out long, and she always returned exhausted. After a while, she gave up going out. "I'll rest," she would say. "Tomorrow I'll be stronger."

She took to phoning people she knew she could count on. The response was surprisingly generous. Then the telephone calls stopped, too. Occasionally, we asked if she would like to go out, or make a call. "Today I am a little tired," she answered with a shrug.

She took no medication except for a painkiller, just as a precaution. Fortunately, she had no pain. But hard as we tried to get her to eat, she had no appetite. Even of the most temptingly prepared food she tasted only a spoonful.

Once she asked why no doctor came to the house to see her. "Maybe he could give me some medication," she said.

I called Doctor Rosenberg and explained the situation. He examined Mamuka and wrote a prescription. As I walked him out he told me, "The pills will not help, but they won't do any harm."

"When my father was very sick and was talking about his eventual demise," Mamuka told us, "the family asked him how they should carry on after he was gone. He said, 'I will not do that, because if any of you finds that he cannot live up to my wishes, he will feel guilty.' But he went on to say, 'I have enough confidence in my children to believe that you will always live up to the high standards of your parents' home.'"

I understood the message, a message for all Jews. We should recognize the effort and sacrifice that go into rearing children, and we should conduct ourselves in a manner befitting our parents' memory.

Mamuka sometimes questioned whether she herself had fulfilled her duty as a daughter. She was pleased when I said, "I'm sure you did." She wanted to be reassured.

Mamuka once said that when she looked at Channah's worried face, she understood how sick she really was. From then on, Channah was never left alone with her. Since Feige and Rivkah worked, that left me to relieve Tatika during the day. I left three-year-old Bela with Miriam, a wonderful, responsible babysitter, and ran back and forth between Mamuka's home and mine countless times each day.

A hospital bed was installed in the living room so that Mamuka would not have to go up and down the stairs. When visitors came, we encouraged her to sit in a chair.

Old Mrs. Hoffman came to visit and asked Mamuka how she was. With a wondering expression on her face, Mamuka said, "The doctor was here, and he may have found what is wrong with me. He gave me some pills."

Whether she really believed it or just wanted to believe it I did not know. There was so much hope in her voice and face that I had to leave the room. I was on the verge of breaking down.

From the beginning, we took turns sleeping on the living room couch at night so Tatika, who was close to eighty, would not be alone with her. One night, when it was my turn to sleep there, I settled down after I thought she was sleeping. After a while, I became aware that she was restless. I turned on a light and set up the chess board.

Mamuka was an avid gamester, but chess was her favorite. That night she argued that I needed my sleep, but she did not put up a very strong argument. She played well and beat me easily. The game went slowly, because we talked about many things as we played. At one point she asked, "Did you let me win?"

Laughing, I retorted, "What made you think I would let anyone win if I could be the victor?"

She laughed quietly along with me, recalling that as a child it was not beyond me to cheat to win.

Shortly, she lapsed into solemnity again. Before I knew it, we were on the subject of death. What she was saying seemed to have been on her mind a long time.

I started to deny. "You have a lot of good years yet. Hashem will help, and you will get well."

It sounded so inadequate to my own ears. She looked at me. For the first time since her illness, we looked each other in the eye honestly, openly. The clown was gone. I could not

195

act anymore, and my tears spilled over.

Very quietly, very slowly, she spoke to me. "Giteleh, my child, this is the way it has to be, not, Heaven forbid, the other way around. Older people have to go. Younger ones ought to live. Unfortunately, very often it does not work that way, but we must accept Hashem's will and not ask questions. There is a reason for everything."

My tears flowed freely. I knew that I should stop her, because it was too much for her. But I let her continue, for I wanted to hear every word.

"I thought there could be nothing more painful than losing one's parents, but I found out differently. I never stop praying that my children should be spared the pain of losing their children."

By this time I was sobbing openly, and she was holding my hand. Gently, she pulled me to her, and with my arms around her frail body, my head lightly resting on her shoulder, I listened.

"People who feel guilty about not doing enough for their parents sometimes scream and carry on at the funeral. My children don't have to feel guilty. You were always good children. You always did more than any parent could want."

At that moment, some of the mischief I had made in my growing years flashed into my mind, and I begged for forgiveness.

After a while, she said gently, "It's late. You'd better get some sleep, because you'll have to go home early to take care of your family."

I put the chess set aside and offered her some warm milk to drink. She took a few sips as a favor to me, and I tucked her in.

"Now I think I'll be able to sleep," she assured me.

I lay motionless on the couch so as not to disturb her. The

next thing I knew, Tatika was gently shaking me by the shoulder to wake me.

That *Rosh Hashanah* was the first one in her life that Mamuka remembered not going to *shul*. Someone came to the house to blow *shofar*, and she made an effort to *daven*. We sisters took turns staying with her and going to *shul*. I would rather not have gone to *shul* at all, but she would have been upset that because of her I was not going.

On *Yom Kippur,* I stayed with Mamuka for *Neilah.* In the white dress that had been part of her wedding attire, she looked ethereal.

Chapter Eleven

AFTER *SUKKOS*, MAMUKA WAS SLIPPING AWAY FROM US QUICKLY. When I walked some visitors out, one said to the other, "Did you see what she looks like?"

After that, the family decided not to let visitors see her anymore. Selfishly, we wanted Mamuka to be remembered for her vital, vibrant self.

Mamuka asked to see her great-grandchild. After the child was taken away, she said, with tears in her eyes, "Shayele would have been a big boy now." Then she whispered, "Please stay together and love each other."

One night, Feige came down just "to see." Tatika heard her footsteps, and he came in also. The three of us sat in the kitchen sharing an orange and talking, then just sitting quietly, with a tremendous feeling of togetherness.

The last days she was able to sit in a chair, we tried to feed her the choice tidbits that people brought in the hope that she might eat. The Satmar Rebbetzin came with some soup she had made herself. When Mamuka refused to take any, there was pain on the *rebbetzin's* face.

In the first days of semi-coma, we still tried to get her to drink. She kept scratching the coverlet restlessly with her fingers.

One day, she opened her eyes and was quite lucid.

"I dreamed," she said, "that I was walking and saw my parents, Avraham Meyer, Chayah Sarah and Raidl coming toward me."

The only one missing was Eisik. She never really accepted the fact that he was gone.

Visitors were still coming, not to Mamuka, but to the kitchen to see us. They told us many stories about Mamuka. One close friend told about the time she was sick with a fever and her four children were driving her out of her mind with their demands. The doorbell rang, and she thought, Company—that's all I need.

It was Mamuka. In a very short time, the children stopped screaming. Mamuka told the mother to lie down, and she herself played with the children. After Mamuka left, the children quietly played at being Mrs. Weinstock.

As hard as it was to make her take the pill, we still gave it to her, for fear she might be in pain. Even when she was in a deep coma, her fingers kept moving restlessly. There was very little we could do for her except to keep her clean and as comfortable as possible. Feige stopped working in order to be there full time. So did we all. It comforted us just to be there together.

A week into her coma, at four o'clock Friday morning, the phone rang, jolting us out of a deep sleep. Mechel answered on the first ring and listened for a short time. When he replaced the receiver, he said, "Get dressed. Feige said something seems to be wrong."

We dressed hurriedly, pulling on our coats on the way out. We ran the three blocks. The rest of the family was there already.

Mamuka was making candle-lighting-type motions with her arms, which she had not moved for nearly a week. She was also making an effort to say something that sounded like "light . . . light . . . " Assuming that the small light burning in the opposite corner was disturbing her, someone turned it off, but she continued in this strange manner. Her breathing was abnormally heavy. Gently, I took her hand in mine. With tears in his eyes, Mechel told me to let go and move away from the bed. I understood. Mamuka was in the throes of death, and we were not allowed to touch her.

Towards six in the morning, she quieted down and seemed to be sleeping peacefully. It seemed as if Hashem was giving her the gift of an extra day of life.

That evening, after candle lighting, we were again sitting in the room, quietly talking. Her condition was the same as in the morning.

Shabbos morning, she was still sleeping, seemingly relaxed. Not realizing how far gone she was, we decided to give her the pill. I slipped my right arm under her shoulder to lift her a little. She opened her eyes. For a bare second it seemed as if she was aware of us. Feige put the pill into her mouth. Rivkah was standing by with a glass of water to spoon in after the pill, but Mamuka turned her head away.

Later in the morning, she began to breathe heavily again. Mechel brought someone from the *chevra kadisha* to give his opinion. He said that the end was coming but it could take hours. Tatika and we sisters sat in the kitchen, listening to Michael recite *Tehillim* in Mamuka's room.

Very slowly, her breathing became quieter and quieter. At 2:30, Michael, wiping his eyes, walked out of the room.

Mamuka had told us that when her father passed away on *Shabbos*, the children were told, "Don't cry; it's *Shabbos*." Now we quietly told each other not to cry.

The news of Mamuka's passing spread very fast. People who came to visit told others. The coming and going seemed unreal.

Motzei Shabbos, we four sisters lifted her off the bed and gently placed her on the floor. The Satmar Rebbetzin phoned to say that Mamuka had wanted eighteen candles lit. Someone was sent to ask the grocer to open up and sell us the candles.

There was majesty about her, even in death, with all those candles burning around her. Hordes of people offered to do *shemirah*.

Sunday was a breathtakingly brilliant blue and gold day. We were taken to the funeral home. Mamuka had said a number of times that she would like to have the *taharah* done in a place where there was a *mikveh*. It bothered her that in the last few years she had not been able to go to the *mikveh* before *Yom Kippur*.

The way Aunt Gitel carried on as she did the *taharah* reminded me of how Raizy had carried on over the loss of her little girl long ago in Apagy.

After the *taharah*, we were taken downstairs for a last look. Mamuka was covered from head to toe, but her hands were folded on top of the sheet. Feige nudged me with her elbow and whispered, "Her hands are at rest." She wanted me to realize that Mamuka was no longer suffering.

I remember the dear, sad face of the Matersdorfer Rebbetzin as she rent our clothes and recited the *berachah* with us. As if in a dream, we got into cars to ride to the

Tzelemer *shul* on Bedford Avenue. Due to a mix-up, we did not pass the house of the Satmar Rebbe, who was left waiting there to join the *levayah*. The *rebbetzin* had already come with us.

There were huge crowds of people—men and women, young mothers pushing baby carriages. The Tzelemer Rav made a short speech. Suddenly, I saw Mechel standing at the *aron* with a letter in his hand. The envelope, which had been found on top of her *tachrichim* in the Beech Nut box, bore the inscription: "To be read at my funeral." A hush fell over the crowd as Mechel slowly started to read. The following are excerpts from that letter:

> Please let no lengthy speeches be made at my funeral.
>
> I declare that from all the money I collected, my family never used a penny, even as a loan. Whenever I collected for a new project, I always took from my husband first, then from my children, and only afterwards did I approach strangers.
>
> If inadvertently I hurt anyone in any way, I ask for forgiveness; and if anyone feels that he might have hurt me, I forgive him.
>
> What hurts me most when I write these lines is the thought of my children suffering as this letter is read.

By now, people were weeping unabashedly.

Someone started a mournful recitation of *Kel Malei Rachamim*. I can still feel the sadness of the crowd. The *aron* was lifted. The Tzelemer Rav, Tatika and the sons-in-law walked right after it, followed by a crowd of men. Behind them came us four sisters, holding onto each other, mindful of Mamuka's last wish to keep together. After a few blocks, I realized that we were heading toward the Tzelemer Yeshivah on South First Street.

Feige whispered to me, "Mamuka would have liked this." Indeed, Mamuka had a great appreciation for beauty. The day was glorious, and the respect paid to her was beautiful even in its sadness.

I had cried so much during Mamuka's illness that I always wore dark glasses in the street because my eyes were perpetually red and painful. Now, despite my deep sorrow, I had no tears.

Someone remarked, "She's not even crying." A friend gave me a hard pinch and admonished, "Cry!" The pinch hurt, but it did not bring the ordered tears.

Four blocks from the *yeshivah*, I saw the children and their *rabbeim* lined up on both sides of the street to pay tribute to this great lady. Their sad child's eyes following the *aron* stirred my heart, and the tears finally began to flow.

Mamuka had collected money from the family to have a *Sefer Torah* written in memory of her children and grandchildren who died *al kiddush Hashem*. It was dedicated at a beautiful *simchah* in New Square. Many of those who attended said, "She is surely smiling in Heaven."